THE CATHOLIC UNIVERSITY OF AMERICA
CANON LAW STUDIES
Number 69

THE IMPEDIMENT OF CRIME

AN HISTORICAL SYNOPSIS AND COMMENTARY

A DISSERTATION

Submitted to the Faculty of Canon Law of the Catholic University of America in Partial Fulfillment of the Requirements for the Degree of

DOCTOR OF CANON LAW

BY

JOHN F. DONOHUE, M.A., J.C.L.
Priest of the Diocese of Buffalo

THE CATHOLIC UNIVERSITY OF AMERICA
WASHINGTON, D. C.
1931

Nihil Obstat:

VALENTINUS SCHAAF, O.F.M., J.C.D.,
Censor Deputatus.

Washingtonii, D. C., die VI Maii, 1931.

Imrimatur:

✠GUILLELMUS TURNER, S.T.D.,
Episcopus Buffalensis.

Buffali, N. Y., die VI Maii, 1931.

35
WASHINGTON TYPOGRAPHERS, INC.
WASHINGTON, D. C.

To

My First Teacher

and

Ceaseless Inspiration

MY MOTHER

TABLE OF CONTENTS

CHAPTER V

CHAPTER VI

FOREWORD

The impediment of crime, not being one of the better known obstacles to matrimony, is oftentimes overlooked, or, to say it more mildly, its presence is less suspected when a couple present themselves for the matrimonial preliminaries, one or other of them having previously been married. In many cases the virtue of continency has been seemingly engulfed in the wave of moral laxity submerging the modern world, and it is not an unusual feature of present-day life to witness married men and women tiring of their connubial privileges and seeking forbidden romance elsewhere. Herein lies the possibility of contracting this impediment in the first of its species, viz., adultery with a promise of marriage or with an attempted marriage.

Conjugicide, with or without adultery, is likewise not an unknown nor an impossible contingency. An Associated Press dispatch of February 22, 1931, contains information to the effect that of the six couples participating in a double execution in the United States since 1873 five couples paid their debt to society because they had murdered the spouse of one of the principals.

It is with the hope of making this impediment better known in all its species, and of fostering a more vigilant alertness on the part of priests preparing couples for marriage, that this treatise has been attempted.

Occasion is here taken to express the gratitude of the writer to Rt. Rev. William Turner, D.D., Bishop of Buffalo, gifted patron of letters and zealous advocate of all scholastic endeavor, for the opportunity of advanced study; to the learned Doctors of the Faculty of the School of Canon Law at the Catholic University of America for their valuable suggestions and continued aid; to Msgr. James H. Murphy, J.C.D. and Rev. Eugene B. Regan of the diocese of Buffalo for their unfailing encouragement and support; and to his priestly companions and friends of Caldwell Hall who have given so generously of their time and ability in the preparation of the manuscripts and proofs, the Reverend Fathers Martin L. McNicholas, J.C.D., Ph.D., Donald J. Gregory, J.U.D., William J. Walsh, Ph.D., J. James Bannon, M.A., and Patrick Dignan, M.A.

Washington, D. C., Feast of St. Monica, May, 1931.

CHAPTER I

CONSIDERATION OF ADULTERY

Art. I. Natural Law

To enter into a complete and exhaustive study of the natural law in its particular relation to adultery is not the purpose of this volume. Such a work would be a study in itself. While it cannot be stated that adultery is definitely contained within the scope of the law of nature, the purpose here is to show that it is indirectly and tacitly contained in that first and highest of all laws.

The natural law, in its generally accepted divisions, has a three-fold classification, viz., moral, physical, and psychological. We shall confine ourselves to the first, i.e., the moral, for we are concerned with the morality alone of the crime in question. The natural moral law is defined as "that part of the eternal law which the Author of Nature makes known to man by means of the nature which He gave him, i.e., reason examining into the trend of man's instincts or natural impulses so as to find out what best fulfills the needs of man's nature, and therefore makes for the maximum of human welfare or human perfection." [1] This law is an inherent something in man—not an innate idea or set of ideas, but a real objective law governing his mode of life, and the natural law of morals is just as basic, just as fundamental as the natural law of motion. It is an objective truth, and pertains in no way to subjective perception. It is a general truth based on nature itself, and capable

[1] Staudt, *Knowableness of the Natural Law.*

of being known by human reason. It looks into the essences of morals, discovering the order between them, and deducing conclusions from these primary intuitions.[2] Victor Cathrein expresses the same opinion in different words, "The natural law is the foundation of all human laws and precepts. . . . Indeed, all human laws and precepts are fundamentally the conclusions, or more minute determinations of the general principles of the natural law."[3] McDonald continually stresses the objective consideration of natural law—"an order or relation objectively existing"—and this is a point to be kept clearly in mind. He refuses to call it "an impression of the divine light on the soul of man," or a conception, or an act of intellect or will, but calls it rather a general truth regarding the objective relations subsisting between the essences of any particular crime.

If this definition of natural law is understood, then it is no difficult task to prove that adultery is inherently condemned by the law of nature. Anyone with belief in a Supreme Being must perforce acknowledge the natural law, for it would be inconceivable to imagine such a Being, lacking in justice, goodness and wisdom, and failing to give such a law. Men everywhere agree that there is a moral law given to guide their actions. In no part of the world can there be found people utterly unable to distinguish between good and evil, virtue and vice. They may not all agree in a question of details, but they do admit a difference between right and wrong And so we may rightfully presume to admit that all men know and are guided by the natural law, for to hold a contrary view "would be to contra-

---

[2] Walter McDonald, "The Natural Law," in Leibell, *Readings in Ethics*, p. 319.

[3] Victor Cathrein, "The Natural Law," in Leibell, *Readings in Ethics*, p. 322.

dict actual facts, to distort history, and to do violence to reason itself."[4]

In general, then, it is safe to say that the precepts of the Decalogue are but particularizations of the natural law given by the Divine Legislator of both these laws, and that they are recognized and observed by practically all men. Thus, men worship either the True God or false gods whom they sincerely believe to be true: they honor their parents; they know it is wrong to steal, to murder, to commit adultery. True, in certain primitive races, such crimes are condoned under what they consider justifiable conditions but, in general, precepts of this kind are universally recognized. Men, even the most savage and untamed, firmly believe in the natural law and its emanation from the Deity, and evidence this by doing their utmost to appease the angered Deity by means of prayer and sacrifice.[5]

Centuries ago St. Thomas Aquinas stated that "all men do know the truth to a certain extent, at least to the extent of the common principles of the natural law," [6] and the statement of the saint has not been disproved up to the present time, in spite of the numerous attempts to do so.

Even before the Mosaic Law was given to the Jewish people, adulterers were punished by death, as can be judged from the Book of Genesis.[7] The Code of Hammurabi (2250 B.C.) punished adultery with drowning.[8] Among the pagans of later times drastic penalties were ordered for this crime. Tiraquelli lists the following

---

[4] Staudt, *Knowableness of the Natural Law.*

[5] Victor Cathrein, "The Natural Law," in Leibell, *Readings in Ethics*, p. 321.

[6] St. Thomas Aquinas, Summa Theologica, Ia, 2ae, p. 93.

[7] *Genesis,* XXVI, 11; XXXVIII.

[8] Law 129.

penalties: Among the Arabians and in the region of Aromatifera, King Tenedius ordered adulterers to be tied together and thus to die, following which a medal was struck, bearing the headsman's axe on one side and the faces of the adulterers on the other, both faces protruding from the same neck The Longobards also had laws punishing adultery with death. Among the Lydians, women who sinned after marriage were offered no hope of pardon, and from the wording of their laws it can be gathered that the punishment of death was inflicted.

Among the Egyptians, anyone taken in adultery was punished with severity, an adulterer receiving a thousand lashes, and an adulteress having her nose cut off. If a man violated a free woman the penalty was castration, because in the one crime three major offenses were included, viz., injury, seduction, and confusion.

In so far as the Egyptian law pertained to women it was intimated by the Sicilians, who also cut off the nose of an adulteress, but followed the Romans in regard to men, punishing the adulterer with castration.

The Parthians punished no crimes more gravely than adultery, and Zaleucus, the legislator of Locra, made a law to the effect that both eyes of any one guilty of adultery should be plucked out. On one occasion, when his own son was taken in adultery, the populace wished to free him on account of his illustrious father, but Zaleucus, at one and the same time a merciful father and just law-giver, ordered that one eye be removed from his son and one from himself.

The people of Leprae seized adulterers and led them around the city for three days, and then for the rest of their lives such men were considered contemptible and infamous. Women taken in adultery were forced to stand for eleven days in the public square, and were then renounced as infamous.

The Athenians forbade adulteresses to enter the public temples, and if they did enter, it was allowed to anyone meeting them to give whatever punishment they pleased, except to inflict death; this latter was not allowed, so that they might longer endure their shame. It was allowed a husband to kill with impunity the man who committed adultery with his wife. In the time of Hippomenes, Prince of Athens, an adulteress was placed in a stall with a horse; the horse was deprived of food and, when hungry, he would bite her. An adulterer was tied to horses and carried thru the entire region of Attica by them and torn to pieces.

The Armenians, Germans, Mahometans, Pisidians, and many other peoples all had their own specific punishments for adultery, some inflicting death by any means, some by stoning and other particular methods, while others dealt with them less severely, ordering floggings and shaming them publicly.

But enough has been said concerning this matter to show that, even tho adultery as such might not be specifically condemned by the natural law, nevertheless, among the peoples guided by no other law there was an abhorrence of it as a despicable crime deserving the severest penalties.[9]

Art. II. Divine Positive Law

The race of men had graced this earth but a comparatively short time before an All-Wise Creator decided to give it a divine positive law, whereby men could better and more confidently work out their eternal destiny. And so we read of Him speaking to His servant Moses amid thunder and lightning on Sinai's heights, and giving to him the two tablets of stone upon

---

[9] Tiraquelli, *De Legibus Connubialibus et Jure Maritali,* glossae primae pars XIII, nn. 6-24.

which were engraved the ten manifestations of His Will, the Commandments, binding men to a strict observance of His Law.[10] Among the precepts, as enumerated, stands the terse and emphatic prohibition, "Thou shalt not commit adultery." This Commandment, in its broader sense and in conjunction with the ninth Commandment, forbids all indecent thoughts, words, and actions, but in its strict sense it prohibits sexual intercourse between two individuals, one or both of whom are lawfully married to another. This evil, apparently existent from the earliest times, received its definite condemnation on Mount Sinai. Later on in the revealed Word there is found a severe penalty attached to the violation of this precept; in fact, it is the supreme penalty of death. The book of Leviticus, the book of Moses which treats of the duties of priests and levites, repeats this penalty: "If any man commit adultery with the wife of another, and defile his neighbor's wife, let them be put to death, both the adulterer and the adulteress." [11] And further on, in the book of Deuteronomy, which repeats and inculcates the ordinances formerly given on Mount Sinai, along with other precepts not previously expressed, the text again condemns this abomination with the words, "If a man lie with another man's wife, they shall both die, the adulterer and the adulteress, and thou shalt take away the evil out of Israel." [12]

Despite the fact that the Almighty had given this solemn command to His people, and despite the fact that the law of that chosen race imposed the supreme penalties upon its violators, David, the anointed king of the nation, is found guilty of its infraction. And not

---

[10] *Exodus*, XX, 1-17.

[11] *Leviticus*, XX, 10.

[12] *Deuteronomy*, XXII, 22.

only that, but his sin carried with it all the conditions later required in ecclesiastical law to constitute a species of the present diriment impediment to marriage, viz., adultery and conjugicide.[13]

Art. III. Ecclesiastical Law

Definite and severe are the prohibitions forbidding the people of God to fall into adultery, and terrible and swift are the punishments meted out for such crimes, as found in the revealed Word. Early in the Book of Genesis Abimelech, king of Gerara, desires adultery with Sara—not knowing she was the wife of Abraham—and the Almighty comes to him in a dream by night and says to him, "Lo, thou shalt die for the woman thou hast taken, for she hath a husband." [14] The narrative of David and Bethsabee has already been mentioned and its consequent punishment was the death of the child conceived in adultery: "for this thing the child that is born of thee shall surely die." [15] The curse of Job upon adulterers is withering in its terror: "Cursed be his portion on the earth; let him not walk by the way of the vineyards. Let him pass thru the snow waters to excessive heat, and his sin even to hell. Let mercy forget him: may worms be his sweetness: let him be remembered no more, but be broken in pieces as an unfruitful tree." [16] The same holy man later calls it "a heinous crime and a most grievous iniquity, a fire that devoureth even to destruction." [17] The Proverbs say that "an adulterer, for the folly of his heart, shall destroy his own soul: he gath-

---

[13] *II Kings,* Chapters XI and XII.

[14] *Genesis,* XX, 3.

[15] *II Kings,* XII, 14.

[16] *Job* XXIV, 18-20.

[17] *Job,* XXXI, 11, 12.

ereth to himself shame and dishonor, and his reproach shall not be blotted out." [18] Wisdom, after extolling the chaste generation, condemns the adulterous: "The multiplied brood of the wicked shall not thrive, and bastard slips shall not take deep root, nor any fast foundation. For the branches not being perfect, shall be broken, and their fruits shall be unprofitable, and sour to eat, and fit for nothing. For the children that are born of unlawful beds are witnesses of wickedness against their parents in their trial." [19] Ecclesiasticus likewise flays the memory of the adulterous, for every man despises his own soul, who "passeth beyond his own bed. And he shall be in disgrace with all men, because he understood not the fear of the Lord. So every woman also that leaveth her husband and bringeth in an heir by another. For first she hath been unfaithful to the law of the Most High; and secondly she hath offended against her husband; thirdly she hath fornicated in adultery, and hath gotten her children of another man. She shall leave her memory to be cursed, and her infamy shall not be blotted out."[20] Finally, St. Paul, writing to the Corinthians, assures them that heaven is not open to adulterers: "Do not err; neither fornicators, nor idolaters, nor adulterers . . . shall possess the kingdom of God." [21]

A full and complete account of the legislation of the Church and the writings of the Fathers, showing how both have condemned adultery, would be too ponderous and too comprehensive a task to attempt within the scope of this work. It is sufficient for our purpose to give but brief quotations from the Councils and the

[18] *Proverbs*, VI, 3, 5, 6.
[19] *Wisdom*, IV, 3, 5, 6.
[20] *Ecclesiasticus*, XXIII, 25, 31, 32, 33, 36.
[21] *I Corinthians*, VI, 9, 10.

Fathers; a somewhat brief and cursory glance thru these treasures of legislation and commentary will give ample proof of the mind of the Church on this subject. St. Ambrose writes, "Let no one be deceived by the laws of men. Every violation is adultery, and is allowed neither to a man nor to a woman. The same purity is demanded from a man as is demanded from his wife. Whoever sins with a woman not his legitimate wife is condemned by the crime of adultery." [22] Pope Innocent I, writing in 405, says that the Christian religion condemns adultery equally in both sexes,[23] while St. Jerome, in writing of the death of Fabiola, states that it is a precept of the Lord that a man may not dismiss his wife except for fornication, and in that case he must remain unmarried, while whatever is prescribed for men also holds for women, and while an adulterous wife may be dismissed, an adulterous husband should not be retained.[24]

St. Augustine quotes a canon of the Council of Carthage, held in the year 407, to the effect that wives or husbands dismissed by the other spouse because of fornication may not be married to another, but should be reconciled or else do penance.[25]

The National Council of Vermerie in 753 forbade future marriage to certain types of adulterers,[26] and the National Gallican Council of Compiegne, held in the year 757, issues the same prohibition for a man committing adultery with his sister-in-law and for a woman guilty of this sin with her father-in-law. In the latter case the man is considered more blameworthy, but the woman is included because of her failure to notify her

---

[22] C. 4, C. XXXII, q. 4.
[23] C. 23, C. XXXII, q. 5.
[24] C. 19, C. XXXII, q. 5.
[25] C. 5, C. XXXII, q. 7.
[26] Canons 2, 10, 12—Hardouin, *Acta Conciliorum,* III, 1990, 1991.

husband.[27] In canon 44 of the Provincial Council of Worms, held in the year 868, adulterers and adulteresses are condemned to do penance for seven years.[28] The Council of Tribur, 895, in canon 46 recommends an adulterous wife to the mercy of her husband, but forbids him to marry another if he refuses to forgive her and re-establish co-habitation, while canon 49 separates those living in adultery, even tho they may have begotten offspring in that state.[29] The Bavarian National Council, held at Altheim in the year 916, in its very first canon denied marriage to accomplices in adultery, and stated that such contemplated marriages were not befitting the religion of Christ,[30] while the Provincial Council of Rouen, 1072, repeats this same ban to partners in adultery in canon 16, and in canon 18 it excommunicates a person who attempts marriage with another before there is manifest proof of the death of the previous spouse.[31]

Letters of Popes of the late twelfth and early thirteenth centuries (all of which will be more specifically treated in the history and commentary of the impediment of crime) state definite penalties for adulterers contemplating further marriage. Pope Alexander III declared null the second marriage attempted by a man while his first wife lived—provided his first marriage was legitimate; and forbade marriage to those who committed adultery and machinated in the death of a previous spouse. Pope Clement III forbade marriage to adulterers who lived together, even after the first wife died, despite the fact that they had co-habitated for a long time and had reared children. But Innocent

---

[27] Canons 8, 10—Hardouin, *Acta Conciliorum,* III, 2003.

[28] Mansi, Sacrorum, *Conciliorum Collectio,* XV, 866.

[29] Hardouin, *Acta Conciliorum,* VIa, 453, 454.

[30] Mansis, *Sacrorum Conciliorum Collectio,* vol. XVIIIa, p. 325.

[31] Hardouin, *Acta Conciliorum,* vol. VIa, p. 1190.

III later allowed marriage to such, if they had neither promised marriage while the first wife was living nor machinated in her death.[32] Clement III further states that a woman separated from her husband on account of adultery loses her dowry.[33]

Such has been the attitude of the Church from the earliest stages of her history, sternly and relentlessly punishing those guilty of this heinous crime, but tempering justice with mercy when such sinners gave evidence of their repentance—and such is still her attitude. In the Code, the Church allows the separation of spouses, when one of them is guilty of the sin of adultery, provided the other has not consented to this sin, given cause to the adulterous one for the commission of it, expressly or tacitly condoned it, or committed the same sin.[34] At the same time she establishes definite penalties for public crimes of adultery, such as exclusion from legitimate ecclesiastical acts, suspensions, declarations of infamy, deprivations of office, and depositions.[35]

---

[32] C. 2, 4, 6, X, *de eo qui duxit, etc.,* IV, 7.

[33] C. 4, *de donationibus,* IV, 19.

[34] Canon 1129.

[35] Canons 2357, § 2 and 2359, § 2.

CHAPTER II

ADULTERY IN ROMAN LAW

The unmarried woman was obliged by the moral law of ancient Rome to abstain from all carnal relations with any man before her marriage, and not to have any after her marriage except with her husband. On the other hand, the man was not subject to the same moral law, save when he violently attacked the chastity of a virgin or the wife of another, thus making himself her accomplice. The observance of this double moral law was secured in Roman Law by the discipline of the "domus," and the domestic tribunal had power to condemn in such a case, even to the supreme penalty; but while this tribunal was, by its very organization, in a situation to repress every attack on chastity committed by Roman women, it could reach only that male accomplice who was "in potestate patris," and even he could only be called to account for his act before the tribunal of his own "domus." It is at least doubtful whether the faculty recognized in some measure by Augustus to kill the accomplice of an adulterous woman goes back to a custom of the republican epoch.[1] Only the domestic tribunal of the state, that of the college of pontiffs which was more elevated than the others, was competent both for women in the power of the state and for their aggressors. Abstracting from this pontifical procedure, the original rigor of the domestic tribunal pertained to the ancient epoch and is more to be conjectured than proven.[2] Even in relation to

[1] Mommsen, *Droit Penal Romain,* Book IV, section VI, p. 414.

[2] Mommsen, *loc. cit.*

daughters of the family, this jurisdiction seems to have rapidly lost ground, and the impossibility of applying the same measure to the two culprits contributed to this non-observance. One can imagine, consequently, that oftentimes the offended one, especially in the case of adultery, exacted justice for himself; the only importance of this vengeance for the penal code was that in those cases where the man guilty of adultery was ill-treated or slain, the procedure of injury or murder, which would have been possible in strict right, frequently remained inefficacious. Since the domestic discipline did not enter into the domain of institutions organized by the state, the public authority had no obligation to seek whether this domestic repression had taken place or not.

Practically, the law of the republic did not occupy itself with attacks on the chastity of women. The decay of political rights and of the capacity of being represented in a private action, which was attached to these immoral acts, as to others which the law did not punish, did not pertain to the penal law.[3] If it is true, and it cannot be proven, that in the ancient religious marriage divorce was only juridically possible for a just motive, this characteristic must have been true above all in the case of adultery. The matrimonial law, such as we know it, and such as it certainly existed already in the last centuries of the republic, gave to each party the faculty of divorce, and did not demand any reason for it. As a matter of fact, the divorced woman could, at the time of her demand for the restitution of the dowry—if she had been the guilty party to the adultery—retain a sixth part of the dowry, whereas for any other act of evil conduct she lost an eighth part. But these rules merely show that already towards the mid-

[3] Mommsen, *op. cit.*, p. 415.

dle of the republic there was not very much severity for immorality. In the penal law of the republic attacks on the chastity of woman play only a secondary role, just as they do in the non-delictual part of the civil law. It is only with difficulty that the private action of *injuria* can be extended within the narrow field of application of the Law of the Twelve Tables. In its later development this action did not belong either to a seduced wife or to a single woman. These latter were deprived of it because of the consent they had given to the crime and because of their complicity. It could not be refused to the relatives offended by that action, i.e., to the father or the husband, but the fine, which was the only possible thing in this case, was not proportionate to the moral offence. Undoubtedly, the republic applied repression to the keeping of public houses, as it did to gambling, by means of public penal procedure. Plautus, as a matter of fact, is aware of a law against prostitution, and the contents of an official list of prostitutes could be used only for the penal law.[4] Leaving out of account the repressive jurisdiction of magistrates over women, they could equally function indirectly of penal action against women of bad reputation. But there were, undoubtedly, exceptional measures for serious cases of public scandal, and they did not re-act, except in a feeble way, against the crimes of impurity. This weak attitude of the republic is in part the cause of the general decay of morals and of the audacious display of vice which then resulted.

But even on the occasion of the great reform of the criminal law which took place during the last century of the republic the legislator did not repress attacks,

[4] Plautus—in *Festus*, Ep., p. 143. "neque muneralem legem neque lenoniam, rogata fuerit necne, flocci aestimo." Cf. also Mommsen, *op. cit.* part I, p. 183, n. 2.

but the legislation of Augustus on marriage comprised the *lex Julia de adulteriis.* This *lex* merely made divorces more difficult,[5] for it applied to attacks on chastity the procedure of accusation and visited them with a criminal penalty. This law is one of the most energetic and durable innovations of penal law which is recorded in history. It continued to be to the end of Roman Law the fundamental law for such crimes.

The law did not take account of faults against chastity, except when committed by a free woman subject to the duty of honesty (*matrona, materfamilias*) and then the repression was always extended to the male accomplice.[6] Slaves of the female sex were not included under this law,[7] but carnal copulation with a female slave was punishable as damage done to the property of another, altho it did not enter into the category of *injuria* and did not come under the *lex Julia.* It was the same for married or unmarried women from whom honesty was not exacted because of their condition of life; such were public women as long as they persisted in their profession, the keepers of bad houses, actresses, those who kept places open to the public, and women living in indecent concubinage.[8] If we abstract from the concubinage of a patron with his freed slave, which was not considered as being improper,[9] such a union, altho permitted in a general way by the law, was not without danger except when it took place with a woman not subject to the precept of chastity.[10] With another person concubinage was not permitted except on the condition that one de-

---

[5] D 38, 11, 1 *in fine.*

[6] D 47, 10, 15, 15; D 48, 5, 14; Cod. 9, 9, 28.

[7] Cod. 9, 9, 24.

[8] D 48, 5, 14, 2; D 48, 5, 11, 2; Cod. 9, 9, 28.

[9] D 23, 2, 41, 1.

[10] D 25, 7, 3; D 25, 7, 1, 1.

clared before witnesses that he took her for his concubine, and by that very fact this woman lost her quality of *matrona.*[11] But the simple fact of leading a dissolute life did not excuse the Roman free woman from the juridic consequences of her offenses against chastity. Impunity was not assured, except by enrolling on the list of public women or by the fact of embracing a profession which gave the same liberty.[12] The paramour did not escape either, unless he could prove that he was deceived as to the condition of the woman.[13] The condition of the culpable man was of no importance; the crime against chastity could be committed even with a slave, while the consequences of adultery committed with a slave were the object of only occasional mention.[14]

The law did not authorize the woman bound by the duty of chastity to have any sexual relations except in marriage or in an equivalent union. The notion of marriage embraced in law not merely the *justae nuptiae,* whether the married persons were Romans or peregrini, but every communion of life in which the persons thus united behaved as married people and observed monogamy, even tho there had not been the *justae nuptiae.* By this term, *justae nuptiae,* the Romans understood the marriage based on the *connubium* of the two parties, i.e., on the right given by the state to the two parties to conclude a matrimonial union producing the civil effects of marriage, especially the transfer of the personal rights of the father to the children in the union and, if the father was a Roman citizen, the subordination of the children to the power of *pater-*

---

[11] D 25, 7, 3; D 48, 5, 14.
[12] D 48, 5, 11, 2.
[13] Cod. 9, 9, 22.
[14] D 48, 5, 34; Cod. 9, 9, 25.

familias. The Roman idea of *justae nuptiae* was not restricted to Roman marriage, for marriage contracted according to the Athenian law was just as valid as that concluded according to the Roman Law.[15] There was no penalty for the *matrimonium injustum,* i.e., for the sexual union identical in every respect with the *justae nuptiae* save this double difference, that the contracting parties did not possess the *jus connubii* and that the children followed the condition of the mother.

Every sexual union outside the limits already mentioned fell under the scope of the penal law. This law repressed sexual intercourse with the unmarried woman, i.e., *stuprum* in the strict sense of the word; but in the philological sense this word was used to denote impurity, whether committed with a married or unmarried woman; wherefore the *lex Julia de adulteriis* used this expression even to designate adultery.[16] The notion of marriage, on which that of adultery was based, must again be taken in the wide sense already indicated. There was adultery even in the case of the violation of a *matrimonium injustum,*[17] or of concubinage. Ulpian admits the action of adultery not only in the case of concubinage, but also in other cases ("si ea sit mulier cum qua incestum commissum est, vel ea quae quamvis uxoris animo haberetur uxor tamen esse non potest.") [18] In the same wide acceptation it was decided that there was no adultery when sexual relations took place with a woman whose divorce was null

---

[15] Mommsen, *Droit Penal Romain,* Book IV, section VI, p. 419, footnote.

[16] D 48, 5, 6, 1; D 48, 5, 35, 1; D 50, 16, 101.

[17] "Sive justa uxor fuit sive injusta accusationem instituere vir poterit."—D 48, 5, 14, 1.

[18] D 48, 5, 14, 4; D 48, 6, 14.

in strict law[19] The *lex Julia* did not refer to the man; on the other hand a later law made carnal intercourse with the fiancee of another equally guilty with adultery.[20] Sexual relations between betrothed persons seem to have always been considered as *stuprum.*[21]

In *stuprum,* as in adultery, it was necessary for the application of the penalty that the persons who had relations were conscious of committing a fault, i.e., assuming that the knowledge of the moral law which forbade such actions was self-evident and that they knew the circumstances of the fact which was the basis of the one or the other crime. The woman, who because of error considered her marriage as dissolved when de facto it still existed, did not commit adultery when she had sexual relations with another man.[22] The sexual union of a man with a married woman whom he thought unmarried was adultery for the woman but not for him. In addition, consummation of the act was required; the mere attempt was only treated as an *injuria.*[23] However, in the latter case the penalty was notably aggravated by the later law. Generally, in the penal law of the Romans, help given to the culpable parties was considered like the crime itself, and the penalty was also applied to him who counseled it.[24]

The process of the crime of adultery presented numerous and important particularities of procedure. The crime, newly introduced among the *judicia publica,* received a special *quaestio* under the presidency of a praetor, but it was undecided whether or not the

[19] D 48, 5, 44.
[20] D 48, 5, 14, 3; Cod. 9, 9, 7.
[21] Mommsen, *Droit Penal Romain,* Book IV, section VI, p. 422.
[22] D 48, 5, 12, 12.
[23] *"Ne quis posthac stuprum adulterium facito."*—D 48, 5, 13.
[24] D 48, 5, 13.

court was to be restricted to Rome alone or was to be extended to all Italy. The remark made by Papinian on the *judicium publicum* in case of adultery proves that this tribunal was still fully active under Septimus Severus, and that of all the *quaestiones* this was the most frequent.[25] It is not unlikely that the Roman tribunals were competent only for procedures of adultery in which at least one of the two defendants was a Roman citizen, and it is probable that the wide notion of marriage was utilized for determining the competence of the tribunal in this respect.

The faculty of exercising action in a case of crime against chastity had in principle, according to the law of Augustus, the same extension as every procedure of *quaestio,* but the general law of preference of persons who raised the accusation in their own interest made this the object of legal arrangement for the case in which the accusation had been preceded by divorce on account of adultery. In such a case, during the sixty days following the divorce the accusation could only be formed first of all by the husband, and after him by the father of the woman.[26] For the exercise of this right of preference account was taken only of the *justae nuptiae,* whilst everywhere else in penal law the wide notion of marriage was adopted. Papinian expressed this rule for marriage concluded in the absence of *connubium.*[27] Ulpian, however, should also be considered here, for he accorded to the man, in relation to the *uxor injusta,* the right to exercise an action but he did not give the privilege which the real spouse enjoys.[28] The exercise of the action was restrained in the case of a married woman, and the violation of an existing

[25] D 1, 21, 1.

[26] D 48, 5, 2, 8.

[27] Coll. 4, 5, 1.

[28] D 48, 5, 14.

marriage did not permit the attempt of a penal action against the woman or against her accomplice.[29] The divorce should always precede this action; and the husband was sometimes even bound to institute it. If the divorced woman lived in a second marriage contracted before the *denuntiatio* of the preceding husband, action was possible, but it had first to be directed against the accomplice of the woman and could not be directed against her, except in so far as the accomplice had been condemned.[30] Excepting this case, the one making the demand had the faculty of taking action at will in the first place against the woman or against the husband, but he could not institute action against both together.[31] If, for any reason, the action became impossible against one of the two parties, that did not at all hinder it from being directed against the other.[32]

The procedure was particularly rigorous in the action of adultery because here the general rule according to which a slave could not give deposition against his master was discarded.[33]

Finally, contrary to the general law, according to which there was no prescription in the case of crime, the action of adultery became extinct by prescription in two ways; (1) all actions based on the *lex Julia* became extinct by the expiration of a delay of five years, counting from the day on which the crime was committed[34]; (2) if there had been a divorce granted because of adultery the action had to be begun within

---

[29] D 48, 5, 12, 10; D 48, 5, 27; Cod. 9, 9, 11.

[30] D 48, 5, 2, pr.

[31] D 48, 5, 16, 9; D 48, 16, 1, 10; Cod. 9, 9, 8.

[32] D 48, 5, 12, 4; D 48, 5, 20, pr. 1.

[33] Mommsen, *Droit Penal Romain,* part II, n. 2.

[34] D 48, 5, 30, 5-8. Note especially n. 6—"melius dicere omnibus admissis ex lege Julia venientibus quinquennium esse praestitutum"; D 48, 5, 12, 4; Cod. 9, 9, 27.

a period of six months from the day on which the crime was committed, if the woman was not married, and from the day of the divorce if she was married.[35] In this delay of six months the first two actions were, as we have said, reserved to the former husband and to the father of the divorced woman.

The penalty incurred in the case of a crime against chastity affected both the woman and the man equally. As regards the ultimate inequality of the moral fault, the law took no account.[36] This penalty was in principle the same for both *stuprum* and *adulterium,* and consisted, according to the *lex Julia,* partly in the relegation and partly in a patrimonial penalty, which was the confiscation of one-half their patrimony if there was a question of a man or an unmarried woman, and the confiscation of a third of the patrimony and one-half of the dowry if there was question of a married woman.[37] For the persons of a lower state, for whom these penalties were not suitable, there was inflicted, according to a later law, corporal punishment.[38] To these penalties there was added for the condemned woman a prohibition of contracting a new marriage.[39] Later on the repression was aggravated still more and, according to the constitution of the third century, adultery was a capital crime. Constantine energetically ordered the exercise of this capital procedure, and Constans even demanded death by submersion or fire.[40] This state of affairs lasted until the end of Roman Law, and even in general amnesties adultery was reg-

---

[35] D 48, 5, 30, 5; Coll. 4, 4, 1; Cod. 9, 9, 6.

[36] Mommsen, *Droit Penal Romain,* Book IV, section VI, p. 426.

[37] Inst. 4, 18, 4.

[38] Inst., *loc. cit.;* D 48, 19, 6, 2.

[39] Mommsen, *Droit Penal Romain,* Book IV, section VI, p. 428, n. 4.

[40] Cod. 2, 4, 18; Cod. 9, 9, 9; Cod. Th. 9, 7, 2, and Cod. Just. 9, 9, 29, 4; Inst. 4, 18, 4; Nov. 134, 10; Cod. Th. 11, 36, 4.

ularly mentioned among the excepted crimes. Justinian prescribed the internment of the adulterous spouse in a convent.[41]

While, in Roman Law, the marriage state was not a perpetual union, in the sense that once entered into it held until the death of one or other of the contracting parties, because entrance into this state and departure from it rested particularly upon the consent of the interested parties, nevertheless, it is found established upon a moral basis, the duty of fidelity being recognized in law, and its violation carrying certain penalties.[42] As has already been seen, adultery was a public crime inflicting capital punishment, but under Justinian this stringent penalty was mitigated to such an extent as to be reduced to more lenient but yet powerful punishments, e.g., to a heavy fine.[43]

An ancient maxim of Roman Law held that marriage should be a free union,[44] but under the Christian influence the laxity and freedom of this maxim was restricted to such an extent that divorce was allowed only on proof that one of the parties had been guilty of gross misconduct.

Adultery was recognized. This is clearly stated in the Justinian Code, wherein it is treated of the case of a Christian taking the spouse of a Jew to wife,[45] and in the Sentences of Paul the possession of a concubine was forbidden when one already had a wife.[46] The commission of adultery was stated in certain cases as a just reason for a man to kill another, when the latter

---

[41] Nov. 117, 8.

[42] Morey, *Outlines of Roman Law*, p. 247.

[43] *Comment. Steph.* in Nov. 22, 79; Nov. 134, 10.

[44] Hunter, *Introduction to Roman Law*, p. 34.

[45] Cod. 1, 9, 6.

[46] *Pauli Sent.*, II, tit. 20.

was found with his wife,[47] and Diocletian decreed that the memory of the commission of adultery before marriage was not blotted out by the subsequent marriage.[48]

If a man divorced his wife on account of adultery—such a procedure being recognized in Roman Law—and such a charge being proven, nevertheless he enjoyed the privilege of again taking her to wife within a period of two years.[49] Indeed, were he knowingly to retain an adulterous wife, he would be held as guilty of being a party to the *lenocinium* (prostitution).[50] If he had suspicions regarding the fidelity of his wife, and these suspicions were established as a reality by three trustworthy witnesses, the power was granted him of taking the life of the despoiler of his wife, even tho they were not actually taken in adultery.[51]

Adultery as an impediment to marriage existed in Roman Law, as is evidenced by a question proposed to Papinian. The eminent jurist was asked whether the accomplices in the crime of adultery could live together as man and wife in legitimate matrimony, such a union being already attempted, and whether the woman, outliving the man, could claim part of his inheritance. His reply was that such a marriage does not stand, and that no part of the inheritance is due her.[52]

But it is in the Novels of Justinian that the impediment is stated very clearly, and this long before ecclesiastical legislators had taken any action in this matter. Justinian states that an attempted marriage of a man with his adulterous accomplice, this taking place

---

[47] Cod. 9, 9, 4.

[48] Cod. 9, 9, 26.

[49] Nov. 134, 10.

[50] *Comment. Steph.* in Nov. 14, 11.

[51] *Comment. Steph.* in Nov. 117, 36.

[52] *"Neque tale matrimonium stare, neque, hereditatis lucrum ad mulierem pertinere."*—D 34, 9, 13.

while her husband is still living or after his demise, does not avail; and he strengthens his sentence by decreeing the punishments to be meted out to both parties, the man to be tortured, and the woman to be chastised and placed in a monastery for the extent of her mortal life, thus denying future marriage to her. The text is quoted in full, as evidence of the influence of Justinian upon the subsequent legislation of the Church in this regard:

> Si quis vero accusatur de adulterio, per proditionem judicum, aut alio quolibet modo a legibus poenas effugerit, et post hoc inveniatur cum muliere, de qua accusatus est, turpiter conversatus, aut in matrimonium accipere eam, et hoc fiat vivente marito, aut post ejus mortem; neque matrimonium valere jubemus; sed eum, qui hoc delinquere praesumpserit: et si prius profugerit, attamen licentiam damus omni judici et comprehendere eum, et post tormenta ultimis suppliciis subjicere; nulla alia excusatione aut probatione facienda: et mulierem castigatam et destrusam monasterio immitti jubemus; et ibi manere in omni tempore propriae vitae: utriusque vero substantiam secundum praedictum ordinem dividi periculo sicut praediximus, tam comitis privatarum, quam judicis loci.[53]

[53] Nov. 134, 10.

CHAPTER III

THE IMPEDIMENT OF CRIME

ART. I. DEFINITION

There is something revolting and disgusting in the thought of accomplices in adultery entering marriage when the way is opened to them by the death of the spouse of one or other or of both, something abhorrent in the marriage of a murderer to the husband or wife of the victim. It is something repellent, not only in the moral code, but also in the code of ethics set up by decent society.

It is not surprising, then, to find in the code of laws of the most perfect organization upon earth, the Roman Catholic Church, a specific law regarding this outrageous attempt to lower the morale of humankind. And thus the Church establishes this species of violation of the moral code as a diriment impediment to marriage. In prohibiting such marriages the Church considers the crime in all its phases, viz., adultery with the promise of later marriage or with an attempted marriage, adultery with conjugicide, and conjugicide by conspiracy without adultery, and condemns them in all. She holds no brief for any thus guilty, and dispenses from this impediment only when the best of reasons are alleged and proven.

The qualified crime of adultery and conjugicide is the only ecclesiastical impediment which is formally designated as "crime," and it is thus called because it is so especially and emphatically opposed to the sanctity of marriage. The word "crime" is not too specific in its meaning, for in its generally accepted determination it is applied to all serious violations of law, but it is expressive, and its terminology has been in vogue for several centuries; St. Raymond and Albertus Magnus used it even in their day.

Adultery is so clearly recognized by the light of reason itself as a grave crime committed against the natural law that almost all peoples, even the barbarians, have punished it with grave penalties. And the marriages of pagans and infidels are recognized by the Church as true and valid marriages—tho non-sacramental.[1] The crime of adultery is attributable to both husband and wife by the law of nature; nevertheless, in the Law of the Romans, the punishments for adultery were established for the woman rather than for the man,[2] and the former was more liable to severe punishments.[3] The singular rigor of Hebrew Law demanded mutual conjugal faith, for there was no selection of persons in the Decalogue, despite the fact that polygamy was permitted to men in the Old Testament and the condition of husband and wife was not the same.

The Church has always and ever reproved this distinction between husband and wife as set down in Roman Law, because not only the wife but also the husband is bound to the observance of the moral law, and adultery is absolutely and unequivocally forbidden by divine positive law. St. Paul states this equality of man and wife in his first Epistle to the Corinthians, when he says, "The wife hath not power of her own body, but the husband. And in like manner the husband also hath not power of his own body, but the

[1] Instr. S. C. S. Off., Dec. 18, 1872 in *Collect. S. C. Prop de Fide*, n. 1300.

[2] Cod. 9, 9, 1.

[3] D 48, 5, 34.

wife,"[4] and this has always been insisted upon by the Church. Among others, there are found Pope Innocent I, in the year 405, saying that the Christian religion condemns adultery equally in both sexes[5]; and Pope Pelagius in the sixth century issuing a warning to the effect that we must not be deceived by human laws, and stating that adultery is allowed to neither men nor women, physical and moral purity being an obligation for both husband and wife.[6]

Art. II. Historical Development

Roman Law prohibited marriage between those who were guilty of adultery, but it did not invalidate such a marriage until long after that law came under the Christian influence at the time of Justinian, in the middle of the sixth century.[7]

Indeed, St. Augustine in the fifth century rather approves marriages of this sort, when he says that after the death of the husband a true marriage may be entered into by the parties to the adultery, thus agreeing with the Roman Law of his time.[8] But Perrone, in his treatise on Christian Marriage, deduces from canon 72 of the Council of Illibertano, held in the years 300-306, what he calls "an inevitable argument to the effect that the Church then established diriment impediments by her own right and contrary to the existing state law"; and he further adds that this was perhaps the first time the Church had attempted to

[4] I Cor., VII, 4.

[5] C. 23, C. XXXII, q. 5.

[6] C. 4, C. XXXII, q. 4.

[7] D 48, 5, 11, No. 13; Nov. 134, 12.

[8] St. Augustine, *De Nuptiis et Concupiscentia,* Lib. I, cap. 10, MPL, vol. XLIV, p. 420.

moderate Christian marriage in a manner opposed to contemporaneous civil law.[9]

It is in this Council that there is first found mention of crime as an impediment to marriage. The Council did not state it as an impediment exactly, but rather as a prohibition, the violation of which entailed the refusal of admittance to the reception of Holy Community. Perrone[10] interprets this refusal as a perpetual excommunication, i.e., for the lifetime of the spouse abandoned by the adulterous party, but the canon itself seems somewhat more lenient. True, it does deny Holy Communion to the delinquents for the time during which the legitimate spouse is living, but not if necessity (*necessitas infirmitatis*) intervenes,[11] and necessity here quite evidently means danger of death or serious illness.

As has already been discovered, accomplices in adultery later attempting marriage were first distinctly forbidden to do so with the consequent nullifying of their marriage by Emperor Justinian.[12] This law was received by the Eastern Church, but not by the Western until a later date.[13] True, in the latter Church there are found certain canons subjecting adulterers who had married to public penance for a specified time and, during this time, all marital relations were forbidden them, but they were allowed the privileges of their state as soon as this penance was performed.

The Council of Frioul of the Western Church, held in the year 796, forbade the marriages of accomplices in adultery to each other or to any third party forever.[14]

---

[9] Perrone, *De Matrimonio Christiano,* vol. III, footnote 78, p. 283.
[10] *Op. cit.,* p. 281.
[11] Conc. Illibert., canon 9—Mansi II, p. 7.
[12] Nov. 134, 12.
[13] Wernz-Vidal, *Jus Matrimoniale,* n. 322.
[14] Conc. Forojuliensis, cap. X—Mansi XIII, p. 849.

In the same Church there is found a decree, called by authors "Pseudo-Gregorian," [15] which allows marriage to a husband surviving an adulterous wife, but forbids it to the latter even after the death of her husband, prescribing a lifetime penance for her. Commentators, however, all agree in stating that at this time the difference between the impediment of crime and what they call "the impediment of penance" was not clearly marked, and that distinct laws nullifying marriage on this account had not as yet been formulated.

It is in the Council of Meaux that there is first found a specific canon definitely establishing crime, as it has come to be understood, as an impediment to marriage. This Council was held in the year 845, and in canon 69 it decrees that an adulterer cannot contract marriage with his accomplice if either of them had any part in the death of the first husband, i.e., if they refuse to fulfill the prescribed penance; but if they perform the penance required, the bishop can then allow them to marry. But from this canon it cannot as yet be fully proven that adultery thus qualified was an impediment distinct from the impediment of penance and truly diriment. It does however bring out very clearly one of the species of crime which has since served as an impediment, viz., adultery joined with conjugicide.[16]

The Council of Tribur (895) first established a true and perpetual impediment arising from the crime of adultery, bringing to notice for the first time the idea of adultery joined with the promise of future marriage after the death of the legitimate spouse. The Council calls such a plan an "execrable thing, to be abhorred by all Catholics," [17] i.e., to have sexual relations with

[15] C. 22, C. XXXII, q. 7.

[16] Mansi, XIV, p. 835.

[17] Conc. Tribur, canon 40—Mansi, XVIII, p. 159.

the wife of another and assure her, by oath, of the intention to take her to wife if she survives her lawful husband. It anathematises such a marriage, and states that it is not allowed and is unbecoming to the Christian religion that one take to wife a woman he has despoiled thru adultery. The same Council, later in the session, again repeats this prohibition and anathema,[18] while in canon 51 it states a direct contradiction to St. Augustine, as he has already been quoted, and says that no one may take to wife a woman with whom he had previously committed adultery.

Pope Alexander III (1159-1181), writing to the Abbot of St. Albans, allows subsequent marriage to adulterers after the death of the spouse, provided that one of the accomplices was ignorant of the existence of this spouse. The same Pontiff forbids marriage to accomplices aware of the existence of a legitimate spouse, and to those who machinated in the death of this spouse.[19]

Gratian says that simple adultery impedes marriage only before the prescribed penance is performed, but he restricts the absolute and perpetual impediment of crime rising from adultery to two cases, viz.: (1) if the machination of death is joined with the adultery, and (2) if, while the innocent spouse is still alive, the promise of later marriage is given to the accomplice in adultery.[20] These two species of the crime of adultery alone are recounted by Peter Lombard in his Book of Sentences,[21] and he is abetted by Roland and Bernard of Pavia, neither of whom as yet admit the third species of this impediment as diriment, viz., adultery with an attempted marriage.

---

[18] Conc. Tribur, cap. III in additione—*Loc. cit.*

[19] C. 1, 2, 3, X, *de eo qui duxit, etc.*, IV, 7.

[20] *Dict. Grat.* post c. 3, C. XXXI, q. 1.

[21] Lib. IV, *Sent.*, dist. 35.

The third species just mentioned was added by Pope Clement III (1187-1191), who gave a decision to a case in the diocese of Meaux, where he forbids the later marriage of a couple already living in adultery as man and wife after a marriage attempted while the legitimate wife of the man is still living.[22] His successor, Pope Celestine III (1191-1198), adheres to the same opinion in writing to the bishop of Lincoln concerning a parallel case.[23]

The same Celestine added another species to the impediment in a letter to the Archbishop of Seno, stating that conjugicide alone, excluding adultery, can nullify a marriage, if both parties machinate in the death of the legitimate spouse.[24]

Innocent III (1198-1216), following the decisions of previous Pontiffs, gave a decree to the Chapter of Messana, wherein he permits a second marriage to an adulterer who had previously attempted it while his first wife was still alive, provided the second wife had known of the existence of the first neither prior to nor following her own marriage.[25] This is in accordance with the requirement that the promise of marriage be mutual, a condition lacking in this particular case.[26]

The same Pope, writing to the bishop of Spoleto, holds for the validity of a marriage contracted by parties guilty of sin with each other while the first wife is still alive, as long as no promise of marriage was previously made.[27]

Finally, Gregory IX (1227-1241), in order to settle all doubts and disputes, declared that the impediment

[22] C. 4, X, *de eo qui duxit, etc.*, IV, 7.

[23] C. 5, X, *de eo qui duxit, etc.*, IV, 7.

[24] C. 1, X, *de conversione infidelium,* III, 33.

[25] C. 7, X, *de eo qui duxit, etc.*, IV, 7.

[26] Cf. next chapter, art. 1, No. 2, Qualities of the Promise.

[27] C. 6, X, *de eo qui duxit, etc.*, IV, 7.

of crime does not arise from the promise alone nor from an attempted marriage alone—thus demanding the conjunction of either the promise or the attempt with adultery—and this decision of his concludes the historical development of crime as a diriment impediment to marriage in ecclesiastical law, for as the impediment was then defined and accepted in the discipline of the Church, so it has been accepted and confirmed and incorporated in the Code, the Council of Trent having refrained from any further legislation on this point.[28]

[28] C. 8, X, *de eo qui duxit, etc.,* IV, 7.

CHAPTER IV

CANON 1075

Valide contrahere nequeunt matrimonium:

1°. Qui, perdurante eodem legitimo matrimonio, adulterium inter se consummarunt et fidem sibi mutuo dederunt de matrimonio ineundo vel ipsum matrimonium, etiam per civilem tantum actum, attentarunt;

2°. Qui, perdurante pariter eodem legitimo matrimonio, adulterium inter se consummarunt eorumque alter coniugicidium patravit;

3°. Qui mutua opera physica vel morali, etiam sine adulterio, mortem coniugi intulerunt.

Holy Mother Church, in establishing this impediment, does so with the intention of protecting and preserving the conjugal faith of the wedded pair, and when she takes away the hope of marriage between the accomplices in adultery and spouse-murder she removes the opportunity and principal reason for the commission of these crimes; therefore, she punishes the accomplices on account of the crime they have committed, because such a crime inflicts a serious injury upon the state of matrimony.[1] Thus it can readily be seen that the Church renders accomplices in a crime of this kind incapable of marriage between themselves,

[1] Suarez, *Tractatus de Legibus,* lib. V, cap. 19, nos. 6-8.

because this would be publicly disgraceful and exceedingly dangerous.[2]

There is a dispute among the commentators as to which is the primary and which the secondary end of the impediment, and whether the impediment is more of an incapability than a punishment or vice versa.[3] In the Code, and also in the old law the impediment is purely and simply an incapability, as are the other matrimonial impediments, and the Church has established it solely for the purpose of obtaining the effects already mentioned. Chelodi teaches that the interpreters of the old law, in order to support themselves by the historic evolution of this impediment, insisted on a twofold principle, viz., that the impediment was induced as an extraordinary punishment and as a protection for the life of the innocent spouse, and he claims that they used this as their criterion of interpretation—which method is today of no avail, because now that the Law of the Decretals has been replaced by the Code no further juridic reason can be recommended.[4] Cappello disputes this point because, as he says, this canon has been taken in its entirety from the old law and, according to Canon 6, 2°, such canons are to be appraised by the authority of the old law and from the received interpretations of approved authors. And he adds that the same reason that then existed is still in force.[5]

Doctrinal interpretation, i.e., made by men who are eminent jurists, exacts specific consideration, and that is what is required by Canon 6, 2°; but while acceding

---

[2] De Smet, *Betrothment and Marriage,* II, 657.

[3] Schmalzgrueber, *Jus Ecclesiasticum Universum,* pars II, tit. VII, n. 55.

[4] Chelodi, *Jus Matrimoniale,* n. 92.

[5] Cappello, *De Sacramentis,* vol. III, n. 499.

to the bidding of this canon and having recourse to the doctrine of approved authors, it is worthy of note that authentic interpretation always remains the guide for the doctrinal.[6]

It is well to keep this point in mind because, as has already been shown, the legislation on the impediment of crime has undergone no substantial change since the time its different species were completed and defined, i.e., since the early part of the thirteenth century.

The impediment of crime may be defined as:—An inability or inaptitude established by ecclesiastical law forbidding a valid entrance into matrimony of those who in certain given circumstances were accomplices in the crime of adultery or conjugicide.[7] The inability of this impediment, however, is only relative, i.e., it exists only between certain determined persons,[8] and then only when these crimes of adultery and conjugicide are qualified, viz., when they possess the qualities and the conditions required by law for contracting the impediment.

For incurring the impediment of crime it is of small import whether the marriage is consummated or only ratified, whether the spouses are living together or separated—but it must be a valid existent marriage. Hence the impediment is lacking if a person, who had been married but whose spouse had died, should fornicate with another, falsely presuming that his or her partner was still alive; likewise, if the marriage which was contracted is for some reason or other invalid, even if the person be ignorant of its invalidity.[9] The reason

[6] Neuberger, *Canon 6, or Relation of Codex to Preceding Legislation,* p. 74.

[7] Cappello, *De Sacramentis,* vol. III, n. 478.

[8] Cappello, *De Sacramentis,* vol. III, n. 196, 3°.

[9] Gasparri, *De Matrimonio,* n. 736; Noldin, *De Sacramentis,* q. 5, art. 8; Sanchez, *De Sancto Matrimonii Sacramento,* lib. VII, disp. LXXIX, n. 30.

for this is that no injury has been inflicted upon the marriage state, even if the guilt of adultery were incurred by reason of an erroneous conscience. If both accomplices are married, each marriage, according to some commentators, should be valid in order that the impediment be incurred, but Cappello states that this opinion lacks foundation both in the old law as well as in the new law of the Code.[10] Hence, if Titius sins with Caia and they both make the promise of future marriage—neither knowing that the other is married—no impediment is contracted, for altho both commit formal adultery, being aware of their own respective marriage, still the sin of both does not formally concur for inflicting injury to one and the same spouse. For this it is required that both have a knowledge of the existing marriage of at least one of the accomplices;[11] and by this it is meant that if both are married it is not necessary that each is aware of the marriage of the other, but it is sufficient that one or the other possess this knowledge; so, e.g., if Titius knows that Caia is married, and Caia does not know that Titius is married, the impediment is incurred nevertheless.[12]

The history of the impediment of crime was concluded in the first part of the thirteenth century, the span of its development being completed in a comparatively short period of about three hundred years, and the pertinent legislation has been taken unchanged from that time into the Code. For the sake of clarity and order, the different species of the impediment shall be treated, not according to the time of their establishment, but rather according to their position in Canon 1075 of the present law.

---

[10] Cappello, *De Sacramentis,* vol. III, n. 481.

[11] Wernz-Vidal, *Jus Matrimoniale,* n. 327; De Smet, *Betrothment and Marriage,* II, 658.

[12] Capello, *De Sacramentis,* vol. III, n. 481.

A perusal of Canon 1075, which establishes the impediment of crime in the Code, gives four species of the impediment:—(1) Adultery with a promise of marriage; (2) Adultery with an attempted marriage; (3) Adultery joined with conjugicide, one or other of the accomplices effecting the death; (4) Conjugicide without adultery, both accomplices being instrumental in inflicting death on the legitimate spouse.

Art. I. Adultery With a Promise of Marriage

Adultery with a promise of marriage is a diriment impediment to a valid marriage, as is clear from the Council of Tribur,[13] and it is a universal opinion that the promise must concur or have some moral continuity with the adultery.[14] If adultery were committed, and then the promise was given only after the marriage had been dissolved by death—for death alone can dissolve a valid marriage [15]—the impediment is not contracted. Likewise, if the promise were made during an existing marriage and the carnal copulation took place after the marriage was dissolved, there would be no impediment forbidding the subsequent marriage, for then the element of adultery would be lacking.[16]

A possible question or supposition may arise here in a given case. Suppose that the promise were made to Martha by John while John was married to Mary, and then, while married to still another, Alice—Mary having died in the meantime—he commits adultery with Martha. If, afterwards, at the death of Alice, he

---

[13] C. 4, C. XXXI, q. 1; Conc. Tribur, canon 40, Mansi, XVIII.

[14] Sanchez, *De Sancto Matrimonii Sacramento,* lib. VII, disp. LXXIX; Reiffenstuel, *Jus Canonicum Universum,* lib. IV, tit. VII, n. 4.

[15] Noldin, *De Sacramentis,* vol. III, de Matr., n. 518.

[16] Synod. Ruthen., anno 1720 in *Coll. Lac.,* tom II, col 43; Reiffenstuel, *Jus Canonicum Universum,* lib. IV, tit. VII, nos. 9, 10.

wishes to marry Martha, would he be prevented from doing so by the impediment? Sanchez does not think so, giving as his reason that the promise was voided by the second marriage, and that adultery alone does not form the impediment.[17] He also holds for the non-existence of the impediment in a case where the promise is made and later retracted before the adultery is committed. If the parties then actually commit adultery and later marry when unhindered by the bond, they do not incur the impediment, provided they did not renew their promise following the adultery.[18]

It matters not whether the promise precedes or follows the adultery, for in either case the impediment is contracted. If, however, the promise precedes adultery it is absolutely necessary that it be not revoked, for otherwise the concurrence necessary for contracting the impediment would be lacking.[19] This obtains even if the promise was revoked by one of the parties only, the other accomplice objecting to the revocation.[20] It is necessary that the revocation be made by words or signs, for a merely internal action does not suffice, because the act of revocation must be known to both accomplices.[21]

It matters not how much time elapses between the adultery and the promise, or the revocation of the latter. If the promise is made before the adultery and revoked after it, the impediment has already been

[17] Sanchez, *De Sancto Matrimonii Sacramento,* lib. VII., disp. LXXIX, n. 6.

[18] Sanchez, *De Sancto Matrimonii Sacramento,* lib. VII, disp. LXXIX, n. 6; Schmalzgruber, *Jus Ecclesiasticum Universum,* pars II, tit. VII, nos. 4, 5, 6.

[19] Capello, *De Sacramentis,* vol. III, n. 480.

[20] Schmalzgrueber, *Jus Ecclesiasticum Universum,* pars II, tit. VII, nn. 8 sq.; Sanchez, *De Sancto Matrimonii Sacramento,* lib. VII, disp. LXXIX, nn. 3 sq.

[21] Capello, *De Sacramentis,* vol. III, n. 480.

incurred.[22] It is not sufficient that the accomplices elope, for example, and live in concubinage while the legitimate spouse is still living, but the promise must be made in view of future true marriage following the death of the spouse.[23]

In this connection Sanchez, in his love for detail, mentions an incident that may arise, viz., when one of the participants in a case of this kind may use a proxy to be his or her representative in the giving or the acceptance of the promise. It is his claim that here also the one represented incurs the impediment, for the intention or desire is just as evident as if he or she actually acted in person.[24]

§1. *Qualities of Adultery*

The adultery must be:—(a) *PERFECT,* i.e., consummated. "Copula perfecta melius, nostro judicio, definiri potest: Actio qua semen verum effunditur modo naturali in vaginam mulieris. Quatuor ergo requiruntur et sufficiunt ad conceptum copulae:—(1) *effusio seminis;* hinc satis non est penetratio vaginae absque seminatione; haec erat potius tactus quidam impudicus, sed non vera copula; (2) *semen verum,* et non humor quicunque prout haberi potest etiam in eunuchis; (3) semen effundi et recipi debet *modo naturali,* scilicet per erectionem membri virilis et penetrationem vaginae; excluditur proinde fecundatio artificialis; (4) effundendum est *in vagina mulieris;* exclusus manet onanismus." [25] Quare copula attentata

[22] Pirhing, *Jus Canonicum,* lib. IV, tit. VII, n. 13.

[23] Sanchez, *De Sancto Matrimonii Sacramento,* lib. VII, disp. LXXIX, n. 2; Gasparri, *De Matrimonio,* vol. I, cap. III, n. 737.

[24] Sanchez, *De Sancto Matrimonii Sacramento,* lib. VII, disp. LXXIX, n. 4.

[25] Cappello, *De Sacramentis,* vol. III, n. 342.

aliique actus impudici impedimentum non inducunt, at si copula habita fuit, praesumitur perfecta in utroque foro.[26] Alii tenent copulam attentatam sufficientem esse, i.e., penetrationem vaginae et exactionem seminis in modo exteriori, because there are many laws which do not require true and perfect adultery, but such a frustration of the seed would seem to shatter the motive of the impediment and tend to make these illicit affairs more frequent, because the adulterers would be inclined to sin more freely, the dangers of the embarrassments of pregnancy being removed.[27] In criminal cases an attempted crime does not suffice for incurring punishment, but a perfect crime is necessary—unless, in the law, the penalty was expressly stated for an attempted crime only.[28] Thus, the impediment does not arise from the exercise of lustful acts of onanism, the expulsion of the seed outside the vagina, for that is not perfect adultery.[29]

(b) *TRUE or MATERIAL,* i.e., objectively adultery really exists, in so far as both accomplices or at least one accomplice is validly married. An estimated marriage does not suffice.[30] It is evident that a valid marriage is required, for if it were invalid then the intercourse is not adultery but fornication. Hence one of the conditions necessary for incurring the impediment is lacking. This was decided by Pope Alexander III, who decreed that a marriage contracted thru fear and later ratified neither tacitly nor expressly does not hinder subsequent marriage between accomplices, be-

---

[26] Wernz-Vidal, *Jus Matrimoniale,* cap. XIII, n. 327.

[27] Reiffenstuel, *Jus Canonicum Universum,* lib. IV, tit. VII, n. 13.

[28] Wernz-Vidal, *Jus Matrimoniale,* cap. XIII, n. 327, footnote 32.

[29] De Smet, *Betrothment and Marriage,* I, 100.

[30] Reiffenstuel, *Jus Canonicum Universum,* lib. IV, tit. VII, n. 8; *Sanchez, De Sancto Matrimonii Sacramento,* lib. VII, disp. LXXIX, n. 30; Schmalzgrueber, *Jus Ecclesiasticum Universum,* pars II, tit. VII, n. 16.

cause the previous marriage is null.[31] And thus, because the first marriage is null, neither the adultery nor the promise occurring during the time of this union is true, nor is there danger of slaying the real spouse,[32] for the simple reason that there is none.

(c) *FORMAL* for both accomplices, i.e., one of the accomplices should know of the existence of the matrimonial bond of the other, so that he or she is aware that not only fornication but also adultery is committed. Otherwise no impediment is incurred.[33]

In regard to the knowledge of the existing marriage preceding or following the promise or the attempted marriage and the adultery, Sanchez applies the following distinction:—A promise given or a marriage attempted before the existing marriage bond is known does not bring about the impediment unless adultery follows upon the revelation of the fact; and when intercourse precedes the knowledge of the bond and the promise or the attempt follows that knowledge, then the impediment is contracted.[34]

Invincible ignorance of the marriage bond excuses from the impediment; as does also vincible ignorance lightly culpable, by which one accomplice reasonably thinks the other unmarried. Ignorance truly affected, however, does not excuse, because affectation of ignorance is fraud (dolus) and in law this is equivalent to knowledge.[35] Whether crass or supine ignorance excuses is a source of controversy, some commentators

---

[31] C 2, X, *de eo qui duxit, etc.*, IV, 7.

[32] Reiffenstuel, *Jus Canonicum Universum,* lib. IV, tit. VII, n. 8; Sanchez, *De Sancto Matrimonii Sacramento,* lib. VII, disp. LXXIX, n. 30.

[33] C 1, X, *de eo qui duxit, etc.*, IV, 7.

[34] Sanchez, *De Sancto Matrimonii Sacramento,* lib. VII, disp. LXXIX, n. 43.

[35] Cf. Cappello, *De Sacramentis,* vol. III, n. 481; Canon 2229, No. 1.

holding and others denying that it does. Thus the impediment cannot be considered as present, for a doubt of law is established.[36] If Titius knows that Caia is married, but only in such a way that they both doubt whether her husband, Sempronius, is alive or not and then, despite this fact, they have intercourse and make the promise, the impediment exists, because Sempronius is presumed to be alive until such time as his death is proven. But if it is afterwards proven that Sempronius is really dead, then the impediment does not exist.[37]

§2. *Qualities of the Promise*

The promise of marriage must be:—(a) *TRUE*, i.e., it must be a promise *proprie dicta,* and a desire or intention of marrying does not suffice, because words expressing such sentiments can hardly be construed as words of promise.[38]

(b) *SERIOUS*, i.e., made with the intention of assuming the obligation of marriage, wherefore a fictitious or false promise does not suffice. This is the common and certain teaching of the commentators. Cerato adds, however, that a fictitious promise is sufficient for suggesting the impediment because this would be considered in the external forum as having been given seriously. "Promissio sit vera ex animo, quamvis ad impedimentum obiiciendum *etiam ficte data* satis esset, quia in foro externo praesumitur data serio." [39] This opinion, according to Capello,[40] is neither

[36] Sanchez, *De Sancto Matrimonii Sacramento,* lib. VII, disp. LXXIX, n. 38; Schmalzgrueber, *Jus Ecclesiasticum Universum,* pars II, tit. VII, n. 11; "Leges, etiam irritantes et inhabilitantes, in dubio juris non urgent." Canon 15.

[37] Sanchez, *De Sancto Matrimonii Sacramento,* lib. VII, disp. LXXIX, n. 36; Gasparri, *De Matrimonio,* n. 736.

[38] Wernz-Vidal, *Jus Matrimoniale,* n. 328.

[39] Cerato, *Matrimonium,* n. 70, 1 B.

[40] De Sacramentis, vol. III, n. 482.

intrinsically nor extrinsically probable; *not intrinsically,* for the canon expressly mentions the promise, "*fidem sibi mutuo,*" and a fictitious promise cannot be considered as true; *not extrinsically,* because the authors who hold this opinion possess only minor authority and are few in number and, as extrinsic authority supposes intrinsic authority and is based on it, if the intrinsic authority is removed there would be a lack of the extrinsic. Some authors, with Sanchez,[41] hold that the impediment arises in both forums if the fictitious promise was not externally manifested, but the common and more probable opinion denies this for the reason already alleged, viz., a fictitious promise cannot be considered a true promise, and this because of the wording of Canon 19—"Leges quae poenam statuunt . . . strictae subsunt interpretationi."

(c) *FREE,* i.e., entirely devoid of the elements of grave fear, fraud, and substantial error, as is clear.[42]

(d) *EXTERNALLY EXPRESSED,* i.e., by some word or sign or in writing by one of the parties and accepted by the other. It is evident that the promise must be made in some external manner, for an internal promise would in no way enlighten the accomplice as to the intention.[43] In the old law commentators commonly held that a true promise was not received as juridical until it was accepted;[44] and in the New Code this is certain, for Canon 1075, 1° demands that the

---

[41] *De Sancto Matrimonii Sacramento,* lib. VII, disp. LXXIX, n. 10.

[42] Wernz-Vidal, *Jus Matrimoniale,* n. 328.

[43] Sanchez, *De Sancto Matrimonii Sacramento,* lib. VII, disp. LXXIX, n. 9.

[44] Gasparri, *De Matrimonio,* n. 737; Pirhing, *Jus Canonicum,* lib. IV, tit. VII, n. 14; Schmalzgrueber, *Jus Ecclesiasticum Universum,* pars. II, tit. VII, n. 20; Sanchez, *De Sancto Matrimonii Sacramento,* lib. VII, disp. LXXIX, n. 7; Reiffenstuel, *Jus Canonicum Universum,* lib. IV, tit. VII, n. 16.

promise be given and accepted, *fidem sibi mutuo dederunt,* and a mutual promise necessarily implies an acceptation and also a re-promise.[45] If, then, one of the parties makes the promise externally the other must also receive it externally unless, in a given case, silence would seem to give consent.[46]

Whether the promise must be accepted expressly or a silent acceptation is sufficient is a matter for dispute among the commentators. One opinion, which Cappello holds as more common and more probable,[47] contends that a silent acceptation of the promise is not sufficient because, in a matter of such importance and under certain circumstances, the silence of the party receiving the promise might be much rather construed as a withholding of consent than as giving assent. But with the doubt of law remaining, the impediment does not stand.[48]

(e) *MUTUAL,* i.e., the promise of one accomplice is met by the re-promise of the other. This point of the mutuality of the promise was for several centuries the basis of a dispute among the commentators, and it was only definitely settled with the advent and promulgation of the Code.

Review of the Disputed Point. Joseph Pejska, C.SS.R., J.C.D., in an article entitled "Das Rückversprechen beim Ehehindernis des Verbrechens,"[49] gives a lengthy and detailed account of the dispute among canonists regarding the mutuality of the promise as considered in the impediment of crime. He separates the canonists into two schools; one school, holding *the stricter opinion,* teaches that it is sufficient for one

[45] Cf. *infra,* "Mutual Promise," p. 49.

[46] Gasparri, *De Matrimonio,* n. 737.

[47] *De Sacramentis,* vol. III, n. 483.

[48] Canon 15.

[49] *Zeitschrift für katholische Theologie,* 26 (1902), 131—

party to make the promise and the other to accept it; the other school, holding *the milder opinion,* is not satisfied with the simple promise and acceptation, but demands the re-promise, making a mutual promise and acceptation necessary in order to incur the impediment.

In founding their opinions, both schools rely on the same sources, all of which seem to favor the stricter opinion, because these sources make mention thruout only of the promise of one party. A glance at the disputed words indicates this: "cui fidem *dederat,*" "sibi fidem *dederit,*" "*Praestiterit* fidem adulterae," "fide data *promisit.*"[50] In all these cases it is well to note that the promise of *both* adulterers is never required. The argument of the first school is that to demand a mutual promise would be to diminish the force of the law. It is evident that the adherents to this opinion depend on the verbality of the law.

The school of the milder opinion demands the re-promise for the essence of the impediment, and it bases its opinion on the teaching that a promise *of marriage* is in question and since a promise without a re-promise is not tenable, there is no reason to abstract from the general requirements in this particular case.

Doctrines of the Question. A comparison between the Gregorian Decretals and the writings of the Fathers brings out a very significant point in one of the sources, viz., that of Innocent III.[51] The compilation of Pope Gregory IX was made by his chaplain and confessor, St. Raymond of Pennafort, who changed the title of this particular letter from "Innocentius III *Capitulo* Spoletano" to "Innocentius III *Episcopo* Spoletano," and therefore perforce changed the opening word from

---

[50] C. 1, 3, 6, 7, 8, X, *de eo qui duxit, etc.,* IV, 7.

[51] C. 6, X, *de eo qui duxit, etc.,* IV, 7; letter n. 103—Migne, *Patrologia Latina,* vol. 214, p. 90.

"Significast*is*" to "Significast*i*." What is more important, he changed "fidem sibi deder*int*" to "fidem sibi dederit," thus making the promise unilateral instead of mutual. Was it his intention to tighten the discipline of the Church by this change? In his *Summa*[52] he expressly teaches that it matters not whether the promise was given by one or both parties, or whether an oath was added or not: "idem est de simplici promissione et de et juramento, quia nomine fidei intelligitur quaelibet promissio, nuda vel non nuda." In all these cases, according to him, there is the diriment impediment:

"Nubant, sive fidem *dent* moechi conjuge vivo,
Sive parent mortem, connubia sunt dirimenda."

The first to offer a different opinion was Richard of Middletown, a famous Franciscan and scholastic of the thirteenth century (Ricardus a Media Villa, doctor solidus fundatissimus). He puts the case in this manner: Is consequent marriage valid if the adulterer makes a promise of marriage to his accomplice and there is no response or acceptation from the latter? According to some, this marriage would be valid following the death of the previous spouse—this opinion being based on the authority of chapter XXIII regarding espousals[53] but impediments are prohibitive measures, and marriages which they do not designate as invalid cannot be doubted as regards their validity, which would be the case in the given question. While Richard offers this different opinion, he does not indicate which opinion he personally held nor does he mention his authorities.[54]

[52] Lib. IV, tit. IX, p. 499.

[53] C. 23, X, *de sponsalibus,* IV, 1.

[54] Quoted by Pejska as *Commentaria in quatuor libros Sentent.,* lib. IV, dist. 35, qu. 4.

The Abbot of Palermo (Abbas Panormitanus) comments on the letter of Innocent III and follows the milder opinion, while St. Antoninus does not adhere to either opinion but suggests consulting the Holy See in the case where no mutual promise exists. Henry Henriques, S.J. (died 1608) was a decided champion of the milder opinion, and to him it is self-evident that a mutual promise is necessary in order to constitute the impediment for the reason that a simple promise has no legal force, despite an oath, and the promise must be so formulated that it is equal to espousals.[55]

A vehement opponent of Henriques was Thomas Sanchez, also of the Society of Jesus, who died in 1610. In his work,[56] he uses terms that sound favorable to the milder opinion, but when he comes to the proper treatment of the question he holds to the more rigorous. His basis is the different shadings of the mutual promise. An unilateral offer, one that is neither accepted nor refused by the other party, e.g., when made by letter, is not a contract, but it contains an element of contract, and is called *pollicitatio.* A true contract is that promise in which a mutual expression of will has taken place, and is called *promissio.* In the contract of the promise it must also be observed whether the intention of the contracting party is to enter the

---

[55] These three authors are quoted by Pejska as follows: Abbas Panormitanus, *Lectura in quinto libros Decretalium; Summa Antonini Archiepiscopi,* pars III, *de statibus,* tit. 1, c. 5; Henriques, *Summa Theologiae Moralis,* lib. XII, c. 14, n. 3: "Si quis adulteratur scienter cum conjuge alterius et praeter adulterium formale fiat *mutuus contractus* per verba de praesenti aut de futuro (quae de se sufficiant ad matrimonium aut mutua sponsalia) sint inhabiles matrimonio . . Item si vir adulterae etiam acceptanti promisit matrimonium, *nec tamen illa promisit, non irritat* matrimonium, quia unius promissio non suffit ad sponsalia, quamvis juramentum intercedat."

[56] *De Sancto Matrimonii Sacramento,* lib. VII, disp. LXXIX, nos. 18-27.

pact with or without obligation. The non-obligating promise is sufficient to make a contract if one person remains silent to the offer of the other, because silence is here interpreted as acceptation; but if the promise places an obligation on both parties, silence is not sufficient, and an expressed acceptation is required.

Sanchez, however, merely offers the arguments of the milder opinion in order that he may disprove them, viz., (1) that the sources suppose mutual consent and an unilateral promise is insufficient for the impediment, and (2) that the impediment is placed as a penalty for both parties, whereas it would not be fair to punish the one who kept silent when the sinful offer was made.

Pejska states that it is not difficult for Sanchez to disprove the arguments, principally because he does not mention the main reason. However, this is the answer of Sanchez: (1) The promise of marriage in the given case must undoubtedly be a contract in order to be valid and licit, and for this a silent acceptation is sufficient, because in the impediment of crime the one adulterer promises marriage to the other without obligation and, as it were, out of gratitude or as a reward for the adultery committed. (2) The acceptation of the offer is equally a crime and equally a penalty for both, the promising party incurring the consequences of the crime directly, the accepting party, indirectly.

Sanchez's own teaching on this point is that no mutual promise is necessary, (1) because the text of chapter six of the source title[57] allows the impediment to become effective if one of the parties intends to kill the spouse or has promised marriage while the previous spouse still lives, "nisi alter eorum in mortem uxoris defunctae fuerit machinatus, vel ea vivente sibi fidem

---

[57] X, *de eo qui duxit, etc.*, IV, 7.

dederit." The expression *alter eorum* indicates that a unilateral promise is sufficient to constitute the impediment. (2) In chapter seven of the same title the murder planned and the promise made are given the same efficacy, and since the murder executed by one party alone constitutes the impediment, the same holds for the promise of marriage. (3) In establishing the impediment the legislator did so for the purpose of safeguarding the life of the innocent spouse, but this danger is no less existent even if only one of the accomplices in adultery promises future marriage. (4) Finally, the sources do not mention the re-promise.

Bellarmine, Lemkuhl, Laymann, and Scherer all incline toward the milder opinion and demand the re-promise, while St. Alphonsus, Pirhing, Schmalzgrueber, and Reiffenstuel adhere to the stricter opinion and hold that a unilateral promise is sufficient.

This dispute has been definitely settled in the Code by the very wording of the Canon establishing the impediment (Canon 1075), wherein the mutual acceptance or re-promise is demanded, "fidem sibi mutuo dederunt."

(f) *PURE or ABSOLUTE,* i.e., without any condition being placed. The promise must be devoid of conditions, for otherwise the impediment does not arise. Sanchez quotes in proof the parallel case of conditioned espousals not producing the impediment of public honesty, as then existent,[58] because such a promise does not produce perfect consent, and if the condition is not fulfilled it is as if there were no actual promise. But a conditional promise may on occasion produce the impediment, for altho it does not imply an obligation for its fulfillment, nevertheless it seems to imply an obligation of not rescinding the original intention, and it manifests the hope of future marriage and of the death

[58] *De Sancto Matrimonii Sacramento,* lib. VI, disp. LXXIX, n. 11.

of the present spouse, the latter being opposed to the spirit of the ecclesiastical law establishing the impediment.

(g) *MATRIMONIAL,* i.e., it should regard the entrance into marriage following the death of the present spouse.[59] Canon 1075 simply speaks of the promise of entering marriage and so nothing contrary to the old law can be clearly deduced from the text of the Code.

Therefore it is not unsafe to state with the great majority of commentators that the promise concerns a marriage to take place following the death of the present spouse, and for these reasons: (1) A correction of the law is odious and we must not refuse to accept the authority of the old law if it agrees with the Code. "In dubium num aliquod canonum praescriptum cum veteri jure discrepet, a veteri jure non est recedendum.[60] (2) Canon 1075, 1° makes a clear distinction between the promise of marriage and an attempted marriage, and a marriage contracted before the death of the legitimate spouse is an attempted marriage, which of itself establishes an impediment. Therefore, unless we admit that the promise refers to a marriage to be contracted following the death of the spouse, we are forced to say that the distinction between the promise and the attempt, as made by the legislation of the Church, is useless.

Noldin aligns himself with Chelodi in opposition to this opinion[61] but, all things considered, Cappello refuses to admit their opinion as even solidly probable.[62] Hence the impediment is not incurred if Titius prom-

---

[59] Gasparri, *De Matrimonio,* n. 737; Schmalzgrueber, *Jus Ecclesiasticum Universum,* pars II, tit. VII, n. 8 sq; Sanchez, *De Sancto Matrimonii Sacramento,* lib. VII, disp. LXXIX, n. 2.

[60] Canon 6, 4°.

[61] Noldin, *De Sacramentis,* vol. III, n. 581, 2, note b.

[62] Cappello, *De Sacramentis,* vol. III, n. 484.

ises marriage to Caia after the period of a month or a year, having then obtained a civil divorce. Unless the contrary is expressed the promise of the adulterous parties is commonly presumed to affect a marriage following the death of the present spouse or spouses; nor is it necessary that this be expressly added to the promise.[63] In the external forum, unless the contrary is proven, the intention and the promise of marriage are always presumed to relate to a future marriage following the death of the spouse or the dissolution of the marriage now existent.[64] A view has been advanced that a promise to contract even a civil marriage is sufficient,[65] and this seems tenable in view of the fact that a civil marriage suffices for the attempted marriage.[66]

(h) *COGNIZANT* of the existing bond, i.e., both accomplices must know that one or the other is already married. If the promise precedes the adultery the question arises whether or not the impediment is contracted if both parties should become aware of the other's marriage only after the promise had been made and before adultery is committed. All commentators agree that the impediment is then contracted if the promise is expressly confirmed, but they disagree as to the existence of the impediment when this confirmation is lacking.

Some profess that the impediment is contracted, because the adultery then committed is a tacit confirmation.[67] Others deny this, because a base promise cannot be easily presumed. Still others make a distinction;

---

[63] Cappello. *loc. cit.*

[64] Vlaming, *Praelectiones Juris Matrimonii,* vol. I, n. 315.

[65] *Th. pr. Quartalschrift* (1923), 294.

[66] Canon 1075, 1°.

[67] Schmalzgrueber, *Jus Ecclesiasticum Universum,* pars II, tit. VII, n. 13; Sanchez, *De Sancto Matrimonii Sacramento,* lib. VII, disp. LXXIX, n. 34.

if the adultery is committed by force of the promise once made and with a hope of future marriage, the impediment is incurred; if the adultery is committed independently of the promise already made, the impediment is not incurred, unless a promise implicitly renewed intervenes. And in so far as the fact is controverted, we repeat the old axiom: "impedimentum dubium est impedimentum nullum."[68]

(i) *SIMPLE.* Whether the promise made by one of the accomplices should be strengthened by an oath, or whether a simple promise suffices, is another question raised by commentators. Some, including Sanchez, hold that an oath is required, and they derive their argument from the words of the canon of the Council of Tribur, "vivente viro suo, juramentum dedisse,"[69] but others hold to the sufficiency of the simple promise, stating that no matter what the species of promise is, it implies a marriage opposed to the spirit of the law, and opens the way to machination in the death of a lawful spouse accompanied by the hope of future marriage.[70]

(j) *UNJUST,* i.e., the promise must be materially and formally injurious to an already existing marriage, for if it were not prejudicial to this marriage and to the innocent spouse still living, it could not constitute an element of crime or qualify the act of adultery, and the reasons for the establishment of the impediment could not be applied. In order that the promise be formally unjust, it is necessary that both parties know of the existence of the same marriage at the moment they

---

[68] Capello, *De Sacramentis,* vol. III, n. 202.

[69] Sanchez, *De Sancto Matrimonii Sacramento,* lib. VII, disp. LXXIX, n. 28.

[70] Barbosa, *Collectanea Doctorum tam Veterum quam Recentiorum in Jus Pontificium Universum,* cap. 1, *De Matr.*, n. 4; Schmalzgrueber, *Jus Ecclesiasticum Universum,* pars II, tit. VII, n. 33.

make the promise, and the promise must be joined, during the existence of the same marriage, with a formal act of adultery. If the promise is made following the sexual intercourse, it supposes knowledge of the marriage; if the promise precedes the intercourse, and has really been made in ignorance of the conjugal bond, it will generally be implicitly renewed and confirmed in the act of adultery afterwards committed with knowledge of the marriage. For material injustice it is necessary to suppose that the spouse still living does not consent to or approve of this subsequent marriage. In regard to this point, De Smet quotes a case of recent date occurring in Bruges. There the man had committed adultery with the sister of his wife and later on, in the presence of his wife, he promised to marry this woman. Not only did his wife permit this, but she also strongly urged him to do so, for the sake of the children.[71]

It is not necessary that this promise be made in writing, as is required of espousals in Canon 1017, §1, and an unwritten promise is not deprived of all canonical effect for, joined with adultery, it constitutes the impediment of crime.[72]

Art. II. Adultery with an Attempted Marriage

By an attempted marriage is understood a marriage invalidly contracted "by words expressing present consent, or by some other sign involving a promise of consent." [73] The attempt itself must be true, i.e., it must be an intelligent act whereby two persons, aware of an existing marriage bond, truly and seriously and

[71] De Smet, *Betrothment and Marriage,* vol. II, p. 133, footnote 4.

[72] De Smet, *loc cit.,* n. 659.

[73] S. C. de Prop. Fid, Jan. 14, 1844. The adultery required for contracting this species of the impediment has already been explained, Cfr., "Qualities of Adultery," in preceding article.

by means of words or signs give an invalid consent to a so-called marriage here and now.[74]

It is not necessary that the attempted marriage take place before the pastor and two witnesses, as is required in the form for valid marriages,[75] but it suffices that it be attempted before a non-Catholic minister or a magistrate—as Canon 1075, 1° expressly states: "per civilem tantum actum"—or by an act entirely private.[76] Publicity, or clandestinity makes no difference here, and even what is known as a civil marriage suffices.[77] And it matters not if the contracting parties are bound by another impediment.[78]

It is not sufficient that the accomplices merely live in concubinage, unless they actually give verbal consent in their present state, or the concubinage itself includes a present promise of marriage. Of itself concubinage does not suffice for contracting the impediment, but in the external forum it is equivalent to an attempted marriage unless otherwise proven.[79]

The knowledge required for this species of the impediment should be the same as that already treated when speaking of the promise, but for contracting the impediment it is sufficient that the accomplice who was ignorant of the marriage bond continue to live in the state of the attempted marriage and commit adultery.[80]

All those who are already validly married and who seek and obtain a civil divorce, and afterwards enter a civil marriage and consummate the latter, incur the impediment by this very fact; therefore, without the

---

[74] Cappello, *De Sacramentis,* vol. III, n. 486.

[75] Canon 1094.

[76] Gasparri, *De Matrimonio,* vol. I, n. 738.

[77] *AAS,* IV (1912), 403.

[78] Wernz-Vidal, *Jus Matrimoniale,* n. 329.

[79] Vlaming, *Praelectiones Juris Matrimonii,* vol. I, n. 318.

[80] Cappello, *De Sacramentis,* vol. III, n. 486 c.

necessary dispensation they cannot enter a valid marriage together when the former marriage is dissolved.[81]

What has already been said concerning the concurrence, revocation, and confirmation in regard to the promise holds also for the attempted marriage.

Art. III. Adultery with Conjugicide

According to Canon 1075, there are three crimes which nullify subsequent marriage. One is a promise or an attempted marriage and adultery concomitant with a legitimate marriage, and this has already been treated; the other two are adultery with machination in the death of the lawful spouse, and conjugicide alone. Therefore, adultery alone does not produce an impediment to a subsequent marriage, but only when accompanied by one or other of these three conditions, as is expressly stated in the Decree of Gratian and the Decretals of Gregory IX.[82] The declarations of Pope Leo and the Council of Alpheum which forbid taking to wife a woman with whom one has already perpetrated adultery, must be understood, says Sanchez, as a prohibition only when accompanied by one of the aforesaid conditions.[83] Alexander III seems to imply this when he says. "Licet autem in canonibus habeatur, ut nullus copulet in matrimonio quam prius polluerat adulterio, et *illam maxime,* cui fidem dederat uxor sua vivente, vel quae machinata est in mortem uxoris."[84]

The reason for the establishment of this species of the impediment, as is evident, is to prevent the murder of a legitimate spouse with the hope of contracting another marriage,[85] and this is a most worthy and just

---

[81] Cappello, *loc. cit.*, n. 486 d.

[82] C. 2, C. XXXI, q. 1; C 6, X, *de eo qui duxit, etc.*, IV, 7.

[83] C. 1, 3, C. XXXI, q. 1; Sanchez, *De Sancto Matrimonii Sacramento,* lib. VII, disp. LXXVIII, n. 1.

[84] C. 1, X, *de eo qui duxit, etc.*, IV, 7.

[85] Gasparri, *De Matrimonio,* n. 730.

motive, for nothing more atrocious can be imagined in the marriage state than the existence of so insidious and diabolical a condition, when wedded life should be an ideal union of man and wife linked in the bond of a most sacred love. Witness, then, the foolishness of the attack of Melancthon, deriding the Church because she has seen fit to introduce this impediment. He quotes the example of King David machinating in the death of Urias in order that he might take Bethsabee, the latter's wife, as his own.[86] It is granted that David did this for it is an historical fact, but this impediment is of strictly ecclesiastical origin, and does not include David in its scope.[87]

The second crime, then, which nullifies matrimony, is that in which adultery concurs with the machination in the death of the legitimate spouse, as is clear from the decision of Alexander III to the bishop of Barano, "si adultera est in mortem uxoris aliquid machinata, sive iste fidem dederit sive non, quod ea defuncta hanc esset ducturus, secundum canones ab ejus consortio perpetuo prohibetur;" [88] from the decision of Innocent III to the bishop of Spoleto (or to the Chapter of Spoleto, as has already been mentioned), "nisi alter eorum in mortem uxoris defunctae fuerit machinatus . . . legitimum judices matrimonium supradictum;" [89] from the decree of Celestine III allowing marriage to accomplices in adultery providing there was no machination in the death of the former spouse, "matrimonium inter hujusmodi personas licite potest

[86] *Melancthonis Opera*, vol. XXI, appendix I, *De Conjugio*, p. 1063.

[87] Mansella, *De Impedimentis Matrimonium Dirimentibus*, cap. IV, art. V, introd.; De Becker, *De Sponsalibus et Matrimonio*, cap. XII, 2 d.

[88] C. 3, X, *de eo qui duxit, etc.*, IV, 7.

[89] C. 6, X, *de eo qui duxit, etc.*, IV, 7.

contrahi, et taliter copulari;"[90] and from the Council of Tribur.[91]

The question naturally arises here as to whether the accomplices together *actually* kill the spouse whose existence is an obex to their marriage, or whether their counsel or mandate alone is sufficient for the contraction of the impediment. Commentators are of the opinion that the counsel or mandate alone suffices, and they prove their opinion from the decree of Celestine III just quoted, wherein it is stated that when a Christian wife does not kill her husband, but machinates with her infidel lover who actually slays him, she too is under the ban of the diriment impediment.[92]

For constituting this species of the impediment then, there is first required adultery with all the qualities already mentioned, viz., it must be perfect, true, and formal. It does not suffice that the marriage of one or the other of the adulterers is known to both, but it is necessary that both are aware of that marriage which is dissolved by conjugicide, and the reason for this is taken from the purpose of the law establishing this impediment, viz., preserving the sanctity of the marriage state. Therefore, the impediment is not incurred if one of the accomplices did not know of the existence of the spouse who was killed.[93]

In regard to conjugicide, the plot (*machinatio*) of death need only be laid by one of the accomplices, because mutual machination is not required.[94] Co-operation of the two parties, however, is required in inflicting the death, as is clear from the decree of Celestine

[90] C. 1, X, *de conversione infidelium,* III, 33.

[91] C. 4, C. XXXI, q. 1.

[92] Sanchez, *De Sancto Matrimonii Sacramento,* lib. VII, disp. LXXVIII, n. 5.

[93] Vlaming, *Praelectiones Juris Matrimonii,* vol. I, n. 320.

[94] Capello, *De Sacramentis,* vol. III, n. 489.

III already quoted, where the Christian wives urge the Saracens to slay their husbands in order that they might be free to marry them (the Saracens), and both parties are declared incapable of marriage and bound by the impediment, altho no mention is made of adultery. But if one party alone, of his own accord, slays the spouse, then the impediment does not exist.[95]

It matters not whether the murderer kills his or her own spouse or the spouse of the accomplice, nor whether the machination used was physical or moral.[96] Some commentators think that the impediment also arises when a man kills his own wife in order that he might take the adulteress to wife or, having an affair with a married woman, kills her husband for the same reason, but in both cases they join the slaying with adultery. In this species of the impediment, however, the conjugicide and the adultery must occur during the same existing marriage. An example quoted by Sanchez will serve to prove this point. He cites the case of adultery following the machination but preceding the death. A man poisons his wife in order that he might marry another with whom he has not as yet committed adultery. If he then does commit adultery with her before the wife dies, he contracts the impediment. If the copula does not take place until after the wife dies, there is no impediment, for such a copula is not adulterous, and adultery is a necessary condition.[97]

The conjugicide must be true, i.e., the slain party must be a true and not a putative spouse, for otherwise it would be merely homicide and not conjugicide, which latter is expressly demanded in the canon.[98] It is quite evident that the marriage must be true, for if it is in-

[95] C. 3, X, *de eo qui duxit, etc.*, IV, 7; c. 5, C. XXXI, q. 1.
[96] Capello, *De Sacramentis*, vol. III, n. 489, n. 1.
[97] Sanchez, *De Sancto Matrimonii Sacramento, loc. cit.* n. 10.
[98] Canon 1075, 2°.

valid, even tho the parties are in good faith, then there is no impediment, for there is no adultery but fornication alone. But a marriage *ratum et non consummatum,* suffices for incurring the impediment, for it is a true marriage.[99]

The conjugicide must also be planned from the point of view of clearing the way for another marriage with the intention of actually slaying the spouse, and thus a murder perpetrated thru cruelty or revenge alone and lacking this intention would not contract the impediment.[100] The Code does not expressly demand this intention, but it is deduced [101] from the purpose of Canon 1075, which is to hinder the slaying of spouses by accomplices who cherish the hope of future marriage.[102]

The death of the innocent spouse must be *actually obtained* by either physical or moral machination, of at least one of the adulterers, thru oneself or by means of another, i.e., by issuing commands, by efficacious advice, by influential pleading, etc., so that a murder attempted and unsuccessful is not sufficient.[103] Physical or moral machination is required, for the impediment is not incurred if death follows from any other cause excepting that instituted by the machinators.[104]

In order to incur the impediment, the machination must result in the death of the innocent spouse; for if

---

[99] Gasparri, *De Matrimonio,* vol. I, n. 733; Pirhing, *Jus Canonicum,* tit. VII, n. 5; Schmalzgrueber, *Jus Ecclesiasticum Universum,* pars II, tit. VII, n. 35; Reiffenstuel, *Jus Canonicum Universum,* lib. IV, tit. VII, n. 8.

[100] Vlaming, *Praelectiones Juris Matrimonii,* vol. I, n. 321.

[101] Canon 18.

[102] Wernz-Vidal, *Jus Matrimoniale,* cap. XIII, n. 324.

[103] Gasparri, *De Matrimonio,* n. 739; Sanchez, *De Sancto Matrimonii Sacramento,* lib. VII, disp. LXXVIII, n. 7.

[104] Schmalzgrueber, *Jus Ecclesiasticum Universum,* pars II, tit. VII, n. 50 sq.

it is not thus effective, then the adulterer and his accomplice may marry after the death of her husband, because the canon stating the impediment manifestly demands that the act of machination be completed, noting, as it does, the words "occidisse notentur."[105]

When it is stated that the counsel or the mandate alone suffices for incurring the impediment, it is meant that the one so counseling or issuing the mandate is, by so doing, actually co-operating in the death of the innocent party;[106] for if the counsel or mandate so given is not effective, because the killer is intent upon his purpose and is not to be swayed by any external influence, and can be stayed by no one; or if the counsel or mandate has been revoked in such a way as to render it ineffective, then the impediment is not incurred, because the death must be the result of the work of *both* accomplices.[107] In order, then, that the machination concurring with the adultery give rise to the impediment, it is required that the accomplices be the true physical or moral cause of the death of the innocent spouse, e.g., by giving poison, by violence, by counseling, commanding, asking, or inducing, in such a way as to cause death. Ratification of approval of the deed, when already performed, is not sufficient, because this does not cause death but merely supposes the deed already done.[108]

Another condition required by the old commentators for contracting the impediment is that the party slain be the legitimate wife, and if the wife kills her husband in order to marry her adulterous accomplice, no impediment hinders them from so doing. Formerly there existed in the Church an impeding impediment called

---

[105] C. 5, C. XXXI, q. 1.

[106] Synod, Prov. Ruthen., a. 1720, *Collec. Lac.*, tom. II, col. 43.

[107] Sanchez, *De Sancto Matrimonii Sacramento, loc. cit.*, n. 7.

[108] Reiffenstuel, *Jus Canonicum Universum*, lib. IV, tit. VII, n. 21.

uxoricide, which treated this topic alone, and it is from this impediment that commentators then drew their arguments. It was their claim that it could not be extended to viricide, or the killing of the husband, because the latter was not of frequent occurrence. Sanchez lists the favorable and unfavorable opinions and aligns himself with the latter group.[109] The arguments of those inclining to the belief that viricide is equally deplorable as uxoricide and is just as liable to the contraction of the impediment are that man and wife are correlated and that the same reason applies to both.[110] Indeed, some of them hold that viricide is a graver crime, because the wife owes reverence and subjection to the man in his position as head of the family. On the other hand, the arguments of those opposing viricide as an impediment claim that the texts of Canon Law establishing it speak of uxoricide alone, that viricide is a rare event, that women are not as prone to murder as the male sex and are more timid, that uxoricide is much more frequent, and that men are bolder and more inclined to this sort of crime. It is for these reasons, then, that they state the impediment embraces only uxoricide.[111]

But while Sanchez supports the latter group and their opinion concerning the impeding impediment of uxoricide, nevertheless, in the diriment impediment of crime he holds to the opposite view, and claims that the impediment is contracted whether the man slays his wife or the woman her husband, as long as this is done with the intention of later contracting marriage with the adulterous accomplice. In proof of this he

---

[109] Sanchez, *De Sancto Matrimonii Sacramento,* lib. VII, disp. LXXVIII, n. 5, 6.

[110] Reiffenstuel, *Jus Canonicum Universum,* lib. IV, tit. VII, n. 9.

[111] Sanchez, *De Sancto Matrimonii Sacramento, loc. cit.,* n. 8.

quotes from a passage in the Decree of Gratian,[112] which treats of both these species of crime, and gives the case of an adultery committed and a marriage then attempted after the death of the innocent spouse—such a marriage being committed with this proviso, "nisi forte *idem aut mulier*, virum, qui mortuus fuerat, *occidisse notentur*." The decree of Celestine III[113] likewise refers to the woman killing her husband, not directly but indirectly, thru the medium of the infidel, and here it does not distinguish, for the impediment is incurred whether it be a man or a woman, as long as the slaying was perpetrated with the view of contracting a future marriage by the accomplices.[114]

The intention required, i.e., of contracting marriage with the accomplice of the adultery, has already been mentioned, but this intention is not required of both adulterers. It is sufficient that it belongs to that accomplice who perpetrates the murder, and neither the old law nor the Code demands the intention of both parties. But the intention must concern marriage with the accomplice and not with any other person, e.g., if Titius, a married man, commits adultery with Caia and then kills his wife in order to wed Bertha (who does not co-operate with him), he does not contract the impediment.[115]

The connection between the adultery and the conjugicide requires certain conditions. *In the first place*, both must be committed during the same legitimate marriage. Thus, if Titius commits adultery with Caia while his wife is still living and then, after his wife's death he marries Bertha and slays her in order to marry Caia—not having sinned with Caia in the meantime—

---

[112] C. 5, C. XXXI, q. 1.
[113] C. 1, X, *de conversione infidelium*, III, 33.
[114] Sanchez, *De Sancto Matrimonii Sacramento*, *loc. cit.*, n. 8.
[115] Sanchez, *De Sancto Matrimonii Sacramento*, *loc. cit.*, n. 18.

the impediment is not incurred. Likewise, if Titius is single and sins with Caia who is married. If later he should marry Bertha and slay her in order to marry Caia, since a widow, there is no impediment.[116]

In the second place, adultery must precede the death of the legitimate spouse because, as has already been said, the conjugicide must possess the intention of marriage with the accomplice in adultery, and after the death of the spouse intercourse would no longer be adultery but only fornication.[117]

The reason for the conjugicide must be the purpose of marrying the accomplice, and if it is done for some other reason the impediment is not incurred. And this must be admitted, even tho it is not expressly stated in the law, for it can be gathered from the context of the Council of Alpheum, and especially from the words "occidisse notentur," [118] for these words denote a malicious infliction of death on the spouse, when such a death occurs so that marriage may be entered into by the accomplices. It can also be gathered from the purpose and reason of the existence of the impediment, which is that one spouse may not deprive the other of life in order to take the accomplice; this reason never obtains if the slaying does not tend to this purpose, and hence the laws establishing the impediment do not extend to such a case.[119] It is sufficient, however, if only one of the accomplices intends to marry, because then the machination and intention concur, and it is nowhere stated that the intention of both parties is demanded.[120]

---

[116] Cappello, *De Sacramentis,* vol. III, n. 491.

[117] Gasparri, *De Matrimonio,* vol. I, n. 739.

[118] C. 5, C. XXXI, q. 1.

[119] Mansella, *De Impedimentis Matrimonium Dirimentibus,* cap. IV, art. V, n. 2.

[120] Sanchez, *De Sancto Matrimonii Sacramento,* lib. VII, disp. LXXVIII, n. 14.

From this condition several conclusions may be deduced:

(a) If a married man says to his accomplice. "If I were not bound by the marriage bond I would take you as my wife," and then, after killing his wife, he does take her, there is no impediment because these words do not contain a promise of future marriage, and machination without the intention of marrying does not produce the impediment.[121]

(b) If the married party and the accomplice kill the innocent spouse by their mutual connivance, not that they may marry but that they may better give vent to their lustful passion, or because otherwise they might be slain themselves by the innocent spouse, or because of any other reason, then the impediment is not incurred because the intention of marrying is absent.[122]

(c) If a man machinates in the death of his wife for the purpose of marrying the adulteress, and the attempted slaying is unsuccessful, but the adulteress kills her for some other motive, without the knowledge of the man and without the intention of marrying him, then too the impediment is not incurred, because the machination of the man was not effective, and the slaying lacked the intention of marriage with the surviving spouse.[123]

(d) If a man kills his wife, intending to marry a woman as yet uncertain, or one of many women, he does not incur the impediment—which he would, if his intention treated of this or that woman or one of many, when they were all expressly intended, for then the impediment would exist with each of these, provided that adultery had occurred in each case. But if the man acted by himself alone in slaying his wife there is

[121] Sanchez, *loc. cit.*, n. 15.
[122] Sanchez, *loc. cit.*, n. 16.
[123] Sanchez, *loc. cit.*, n. 17.

no impediment. Therefore, if he slew his wife just in order to marry another *undetermined* woman, he can afterwards take any woman whomsoever, either her with whom he committed adultery while his wife was still living, or one of a determined many, because with the latter the adultery requisite for contracting the impediment is lacking, and with the former the intention of marrying is absent. If, however, he had expressly intended the adulteress in his mind, the impediment exists, because the adultery and the intention are both present.[124]

Sanchez warns against the granting of a dispensation in this case, when the impediment is apparent in the external forum, altho in the internal forum it is clear that the intention was not present, and he advises that the ecclesiastical judge should not grant it and should stand by the presumption of the external forum until such time as the weight of circumstances proves it otherwise.[125]

It is the common opinion that the impediment is incurred even if the adultery follows the machination of death, as long as it precedes the death itself. The majority of commentators hold for both physical and moral machination, so that if the cause of the death was placed before the adultery was committed and did not take effect until after its commission the impediment is incurred.[126]

Others deny the necessity of physical machination and hold only for the moral. According to these latter, if adultery is committed after physical machination, e.g., after a deadly wound has been inflicted or a poison

---

[124] Sanchez, *loc. cit.*, n. 18.

[125] Sanchez, *loc. cit.*, n. 19.

[126] Schmalzgrueber, *Jus Ecclesiasticum Universum*, pars. II, tit. VII, n. 51.

consumed, and death has not as yet been actually obtained, the impediment is not incurred.[127]

Cappello favors this opinion and calls it more probable for the following reasons which he alleges: (a) because this entire condition is superfluous if the first opinion is admitted, and the intercourse would not be adultery but fornication if it followed the death of the innocent spouse; (b) because the conjugicide was actually committed, not in that moment in which the spouse died, but when the act was placed which caused the death; (c) because the adultery which followed the act eventually causing death exerted no actual influence over the death, and this impediment was established in order to prevent adultery from causing death to an innocent spouse.[128] Otherwise, as the controversy stands, it is clear that the impediment does not exist, so that if Titius, having given poison to his wife, then commits adultery with Caia, he can afterward marry her following the death of his wife.

In the third place, the spouse to be slain must be the same one who was alive at the time the adultery was committed, and no other; for the law of the Church does not extend to other cases, but speaks merely of this case.[129]

Art. IV. Conjugicide Alone

In regard to the intervention of adultery with machination, the old commentators held different opinions, some requiring adultery with conjugicide, some requiring conjugicide alone. Both opinions have been ac-

---

[127] Vlaming, *Praelectiones Juris Matrimonii,* vol. I, n. 322.

[128] Cappello, *De Sacramentis,* vol. III, n. 492.

[129] S. C. C. *Neapolitana,* March 26, 1746—*Thesaurus Resolutionum Sacrae Congregationis Concilii,* 1746, 144; Cappello, *De Sacramentis,* vol. III, n. 493.

cepted and incorporated in the Code. It is sufficient that the conjugicide be performed with the view of contracting marriage, for the canons establishing this impediment, while they almost always mention adulterers, nevertheless they nowhere strictly require adultery, and the decree of Celestine III itself makes no mention of it. Thus, since this impediment was established to frustrate attempted conjugicides for the purpose of marriage, it is reasonable to claim that the impediment arises from conjugicide alone without adultery.[130]

Wherefore, when the diriment impediment of crime is incurred by means of conjugicide alone, three conditions are required:

(a) *TRUE MURDER,* i.e., the spouse must be actually slain, and thus conjugicide merely attempted does not suffice, nor does a case of mistaken identity, viz., when some third person is slain thru error—even tho the murderer had the intention of killing the innocent spouse.[131] It is likewise necessary that the marriage be valid, whether consummated or only *ratum;* and a putative marriage does not suffice, even tho both parties are in good faith and they and all others think the marriage valid, because only those are true spouses who have *validly* contracted marriage, and murder in this case would inflict no injury on the marriage state, because the state is non-existent.[132] It matters not whether the husband with his accomplice kills the wife or the wife with her accomplice kills the husband, for

---

[130] Bertachini, *Repertorium Joannis Bertachini,* pars III, p. 331; Reiffenstuel, *Jus Canonicum Universum,* lib. IV, tit. VII, n. 18.

[131] Gasparri, *De Matrimonio,* vol. I, n. 733; Schmalzgrueber, *Jus Ecclesiasticum Universum,* pars II, tit. VII, n. 54; Sanchez, *De Sancto Matrimonii Sacramento,* lib. VII, disp. LXXVIII, n. 7; Reinffenstuel, *Jus Canonicum Universum,* lib. IV, tit. VII, n. 22 sq.

[132] Gasparri, *De Matrimonio,* vol. I, n. 733; Sanchez, *loc. cit.,* n. 20.

husband and wife are held equally responsible by both the divine and the ecclesiastical laws.[133]

The opinions of some commentators who hold only the husband responsible are of no avail, for the impediment of uxoricide has long since become antiquated.

(b) *MUTUAL CO-OPERATION*, i.e., both accomplices actually, efficaciously, and with mutual counsel concur in inflicting death on the innocent spouse. The action placed by them must be fatal, and if death does not follow precisely from their act but from some other cause the impediment is not incurred. The co-operation applied must be either physical or moral, as it is expressly stated in the canon, "mutua opera physica vel morali." [134] Physical co-operation is had when the accomplices place a physical act and cause a physical effect. Moral co-operation is had when an accomplice efficaciously moves some third party to act, either by mandate, counsel, or plea, e.g., if Titius persuades Sempronius to slay his wife, and does this by commanding or bribing him, etc. . . . It is absolutely necessary that this moral co-operation be efficacious, so that both accomplices may be considered guilty principals.[135]

If the mandate, counsel, etc., is revoked the co-operation requisite for contracting the impediment is lacking, as has already been said. If one accomplice merely approves or ratifies the murder after it has been committed, the impediment is again lacking, because the approval or ratification of a deed already performed has no direct influence over it, and in this case the machination of both accomplices demanded by law is absent.[136]

---

[133] Cappello, *De Sacramentis,* vol. III, n. 494.

[134] Canon 1075, 3°.

[135] Cappello, *De Sacramentis,* vol. III, n. 495.

[136] Gasparri, *De Matrimonio,* vol. I, n. 733; Sanchez, *De Sancto Matrimonii Sacramento,* lib. VII, disp. LXXVIII, n. 5 sq.

Whether or not the impediment is contracted if one accomplice consents to or approves the murder about to be perpetrated by the other is a matter of dispute. As has already been proven, it is certain that if one accomplice manifests his intention of slaying the innocent spouse, the impediment is not incurred if the other neither approves nor disapproves the plan and retains silence, even if internal consent is given. If the consent or approval efficaciously influences the act of murder—a point not to be readily admitted—then the impediment is incurred; otherwise it is not incurred because the expressed requirement of Canon 1075, 3°, is not present, viz., co-operation. If the man alone, or the woman alone, or both together without mutual consent commit the murder of the innocent spouse, then the impediment does not arise from conjugicide alone because the co-operation demanded is again wanting.[137]

(c) *MATRIMONIAL INTENT*, i.e., the conjugicide must be perpetrated with the intention of marrying the accomplice, or of marrying one of many accomplices if there are more than one.[138] This condition is not laid down in distinct terms in the Code but, as the commentators all teach, it is manifestly deduced from the purpose of this impediment, which was established by the Church to block the way to another marriage thru the medium of murder.[139]

Therefore the impediment is not incurred if death is inflicted on the spouse thru the motives of anger or re-

[137] Sanchez, *De Sancto Matrimonii Sacramento, loc. cit.*, n. 6 sq; Wernz-Vidal, *Jus Matrimoniale*, n. 331; Schmalzgrueber, *Jus Ecclesiasticum Universum*, loc. cit., n. 55.

[138] Reiffenstuel, *Jus Canonicum Universum, loc. cit.*, n. 24; Sanchez, *De Sancto Matrimonii Sacramento, loc. cit.*, n. 13.

[139] Thomas Aquinas in IV, disp. 37, art. 2; Gasparri, *De Matrimonio*, vol. I, n. 733; Sanchez, *De Sancto Matrimonii Sacramento, loc. cit.*, n. 13.

venge or for the purpose of obtaining the legacy, etc.[140] This is also true if the murder is committed in order that the slayer may wed some person other than the accomplice, and even if the intention of marrying the accomplice should be engendered after the slaying takes place—for, keeping in mind the intention of the law, this intention must precede the murder in order to influence the conjugicide.[141]

In regard to the intention, there is a controversy among commentators. The more common opinion holds that the intention of contracting marriage is required only on the part of one accomplice because, as they say, this is sufficient to present the opportunity of machination, for the avoidance of which the impediment was established.[142] The opposing opinion claims that both must possess this intention, which follows from the mutual conspiracy required and from the purpose of the law itself.[143]

Cappello hesitates to call this latter opinion improbable, because the reason alleged against it is not too conclusive.[144] Wernz holds that this opinion has no foundation in law, for it is nowhere stated that the intention of both parties is required. Besides, he says, the purpose of the law consists in this, viz., to prevent the occasion of machinating in the death of the lawful spouse from presenting itself, which occasion is sufficiently to be presumed if only one of the machinators has, in the machination, the intention of marrying the accomplice.[145] Cappello is inclined to disagree with

[140] Wernz-Vidal, *Jus Matrimoniale*, n. 332.

[141] Cappello, *De Sacramentis*, vol. III, n. 496.

[142] Gasparri, *De Matrimonio*, vol. I, n. 733; Wernz, *Jus Decretalium*, tit. XXIII, n. 528, III; Sanchez, *De Sancto Matrimonii Sacramento, loc. cit.*, n. 14.

[143] Vlaming, *Praelectiones Juris Matrimonii*, vol. I, n. 324.

[144] Cappello, *De Sacramentis*, vol. III, n. 497.

[145] Wernz, *Jus Decretalium*, vol. V, n. 528, footnote 55.

Wernz on this point, and holds that the opinion of the latter is likewise valueless because the law does not expressly require the intention of one party alone, and from the argument of Wernz he would deduce that no intention is required of either accomplice, as long as the law itself is silent on the matter. He further states that no peremptory argument can be drawn from the purpose of the law in favor of the opinion of Wernz because, as he says, the occasion of machinating in the death of the innocent spouse cannot be gathered with certainty from the intention of one accomplice alone.[146]

There is also a disputed point among the commentators on the question of the manifestation of the intention. Many demand that the intention be manifested exteriorly and to the accomplice; some hold that the manifestation need not be made to the accomplice, but to any other person and in any manner; while still others deny the necessity of any manifestation.[147] But the point is doubtful with a doubt of law and to quote the old axiom again, "impedimentum dubium est impedimentum nullum." [148]

St. Alphonsus rightly advises that it is not necessary for the manifestation to be made orally or in writing, and he says that if it is made by means of signs, love letters, familiarities, etc., this is a sufficient indication of it.[149] In the external forum, unless the contrary is proven, it is always presumed that machination in the death of the innocent spouse was done with the inten-

[146] Cappello, *De Sacramentis,* vol. III, n. 497.

[147] Noldin, *De Sacramentis,* n. 583, 2; Gasparri, *De Matrimonio,* vol. I, n. 733; Sanchez, *De Sancto Matrimonii Sacramento, loc. cit.*, nos. 14, 18; St. Alphonsus, *Theol. Mor.,* lib. VI, n. 1034; Vlaming, *Praelectiones Juris Matrimonii,* vol. I, n. 325; Schmalzgrueber, *Jus Ecclesiasticum Universum, loc. cit.,* n. 55.

[148] Cappello, *De Sacramentis,* vol. III, cap. IV, art. 1, n. 202; cf. Canon 15.

[149] St. Alphonsus, *Theol. Mor.,* lib. VI, n. 1034.

tion of marrying the accomplice, if both accomplices concur in inflicting the death.[150]

Some, notably Gasparri, deny or seem to deny this presumption,[151] but Capello states that their claims cannot be accepted—if they really do deny it—for, in the case of conjugicide committed by accomplices mutually co-operating, the presumption is completely obvious and manifested (especially if such accomplices marry soon after the conjugicide has been committed), because it is gathered both from the very nature of the thing and from the viewpoint of circumstantial evidence; it is the lesson taught by experience that conjugicide committed by accomplices is always or almost always done in order that the accomplices themselves may be free to wed.[152]

This presumption is always sustained, unless the contrary is established and proven,[153] because the burden of proof is on the murderers and it is their obligation to prove the contrary. Therefore in the external forum the impediment is considered as incurred, unless the accomplices succeed in establishing their innocence.[154]

---

[150] Vlaming, *Praelectiones Juris Matrimonii,* vol. I, n. 325; Wernz, *Jus Decretalium,* vol. V, n. 528, III; Sanchez, *De Sancto Matrimonii Sacramento, loc. cit.*, n. 19; Schmalzgrueber, *Jus Ecclesiasticum Universum, loc. cit.*, n. 55.

[151] Gasparri, *De Matrimonio,* vol. I, n. 733.

[152] Cappello, *De Sacramentis,* vol. III, n. 498.

[153] S. C. C. in *causa Ulyssobonen—Thesaurus Resolutionum Sacrae Congregationis Concilii,* 1726, Sept. 28, 1726; Wernz, *Jus Decretalium,* vol. V, n. 528, footnote 52.

[154] Cappello, *De Sacramentis,* vol. III, n. 498.

CHAPTER V

PROOFS REQUIRED FOR ESTABLISHING NULLITY AND INVALIDITY

Proofs, according to the commentators, are manifestations of doubtful and controverted things made to a judge by means of legitimate argument.[1] The proofs to be considered are not physical or metaphysical proofs, those which hold in the natural laws or are derived from first principles and conclusions, but moral proofs, i.e., those which can produce persuasion.[2] Facts are the only object of judicial proof, and they must be truly contentious and capable of being the basis for a decision.[3] Notorious facts, facts presumed by law, and facts asserted by one of the contestants in a suit and admitted by the other, do not need proof;[4] while the burden of proving any fact rests upon the party who asserts it.[5]

Matrimonial cases enjoy the favor of law, as stated in the Code,[6] and when a doubt exists the marriage is still considered valid, except in a case concerning the *privilegium fidei.*[7] The favor of law consists in this, that a marriage once celebrated is considered as valid until such time as it is proven otherwise; whether the exist-

[1] Lega, *Praelectiones de Judiciis Ecclesiasticis,* lib. I, vol. 1, 434 and 519; Roberti, *De Processibus,* n. 324; Wernz-Vidal, *De Processibus,* n. 432.

[2] Roberti, *De Processibus,* n. 324.

[3] Wernz-Vidal, *De Processibus,* n. 437.

[4] Canon 1747.

[5] Canon 1748, § 1.

[6] Canon 1014; cf. also *DRR,* vol. V, dec. XVI, n. 17.

[7] Canon 1127.

ing doubt be a doubt of law or a doubt of fact matters not.

In matrimonial cases of nullity there is question not merely of the rights of the married couple, but also of the marriage bond; and, once a marriage has been contracted according to the prescribed form,[8] the presumption is always in favor of its validity. Anyone wishing to have a marriage annulled, once it has been contracted, must prove the nullity clearly and fully.[9] Not only the married couple but also the Promoter of Justice may accuse the marriage and demand its annulment. All others, including blood-relatives, have no right to accuse the marriage, but they may inform the Ordinary or the Promoter of Justice of its nullity.[10]

In the particular case of the impediment of crime the element of adultery is very difficult to prove. Pope Celestine III decreed that the testimony establishing the fact of intercourse (in this particular impediment it is adultery) must be given by eye-witnesses or ear-witnesses and be supported by violent presumptions.[11]

---

[8] Canons 1094-1104.

[9] Smith, *Elements of Ecclesiastical Law,* vol. II, chap. VI, art. V, § 4.

[10] Canon 1971: § 1. Habiles ad accusandum sunt: 1°. Conjuges, in omnibus causis separationis et nullitatis, nisi ipsi fuerint impedimenti causa; 2°. Promotor justitiae in impedimentis natura sua publicis. § 2. Reliqui omnes, etsi consanguinei, non habent jus matrimonia accusandi, sed tantummodo nullitatem matrimonii Ordinario vel promotori justitiae denuntiandi.

[11] "Praeterea quum quis accusatur aliquam cognivisse, an sint testes interrogandi de visu, aut sola viciniae fama sufficiat, vel si iuratis testibus sit credendum, qui se carnalis copulae conscios esse fatentur, sed de visu nihil affirmant, nos inter alia consulere voluisti. Ad haec itaque respondemus, quod, si testimonium conveniens de visu reddatur, vel etiam de auditu, et praesumptionem violentam fama consentiens subministret, ac alia legitima adminicula suffragentur eidem standum est testimonio iuratorum. Etenim circumspectus judex atque discretus iuxta illud, quod in iure civili cautum exsistit, motum animi sui ex argumentis et testimoniis, quae rei aptiora esse compererit, confirmabit." C. 27, X *de test. et attest.,* II, 20.

According to the Code a presumption is a probable conjecture concerning an uncertain thing.[12] These presumptions must be reasonable, and must be gathered from argumentations and indications which, under the circumstances, *frequently happen,* and in cases which from their nature are difficult of proof, e.g., in adultery, the proof is admitted by law thru presumptions which can of themselves produce moral certitude.[13] Moreover, this moral certitude, gathered from the proven facts of the case, is demanded of the judge before he pronounces sentence.[14]

Certain decisions of the Rota and of the Congregation of the Council regarding the impediment of crime are herein set forth in order to show the proofs required and the testimony accepted.

A decision of the Rota, June 21, 1697, requires for the invalidation of a marriage entered into when a promise of future marriage was made while the first husband was still alive a most certain proof of this promise, as well as a reciprocal acceptation of the same. "Matrimony cannot be entered into by those who, along with a promise of marriage, have stained the marriage-bed with adultery, as was defined in the ancient Council of Tribur . . . and in no way is there required for this a conclusive proof of the preceding promise, as in criminal cases, nor are witnesses admitted who are known by other exceptions to be valueless. Indeed, full proof is desired in the present hypothesis, because the witnesses adduced for this only give testimony concerning what has been heard from Pascal himself, the first husband, and hence they make no legal claim for themselves as individuals, altho they are supplied

[12] Canon 1825, § 1.

[13] *DRR,* vol. dec. XXXIV, n. 11; *Ibidem,* vol. IX, dec. XXX, n. 4.

[14] Canon 1869, §§ 1 and 2.

from a number and should be rejected, as determined in a former decision of the Rota. Indeed, since they give testimony only of the boastful threat of Michael (the accomplice), to enter the marriage in question the requisites necessary for the aforesaid impediment cannot be said to be sufficiently proven from this, because for contracting the impediment not any kind of promise is sufficient, but, only that which arises from certain faith and is seriously believed and accepted by the other party to the adultery, as noted in the canons. . . ."[15]

A man who slew his wife because she had been guilty of adultery, altho he had himself been guilty of the same sin, was permitted to marry his accomplice, for it was proven that he slew his wife for the *sole* purpose of avenging her sin. The Sacred Congregation of the Council empowered the Ordinary in this case to permit or forbid the marriage, as long as with the oath of the man protesting the motive of revenge alone there were other *presumptions, conjectures,* or *proofs* which showed that the conjugicide proceeded from the motive of revenge alone.[16]

In a case of adultery and machination in the death by poisoning, the Sacred Congregation of the Council cited the Promotor Fiscalis and the father of the pretended spouse and resolved that the marriage was valid, as supported by the proofs.

This is an interesting case of the impediment of crime based on adultery with the promise of marriage and the death of the spouse. The bishop had established the existence of the impediment but the parties appealed the case to Rome. Twelve witnesses testified

---

[15] *Decisiones Sacrae Rotae Romanae,* vol. V (1), dec. CCXCIX, nn. 17-20.

[16] S. C. C. *in causa Ulyssobonen,* Sept. 28, 1726—*Thesaurus Resolutionum Sacrae Congregationis Concilii,* vol. III, p. 366.

to the fact of adultery, which they argued from *continuous and shameful co-habitation;* seven of these witnesses added that adultery *was committed* and the promise of marriage *given,* and they testified *to having heard,* after the death of the man, of the machination and of the poison placed in a medicinal potion, so that the sick man died the following night. One heard it from *an extra-judicial confession* made to him by the woman herself, and another stated that the man now dead would not on a previous occasion drink the poison prepared by the wife. Against this testimony the defense took many exceptions, and as further proof produced four women of the neighborhood who stated they *had never heard the promise* of marriage given; two doctors and a surgeon who took care of the sick man *deposed in a formal examination* that he had died rather from an innate poisoning than from a poisoned potion. Other witnesses were also brought forth who denied this asserted rumor of the poisoned drink, which rumor they claimed *arose for the first time* only after the petitioners planned to contract their marriage. Then also there was shown *the testimony of the notary* of the lay Curia stating that there was no inquisition in his tribunal against the petitioners. Having heard all the testimony and weighed the proofs supporting it, the Sacred Congregation of the Council did not uphold the invalidity of the marriage.[17]

There is another case in which *Raymundus,* a single man, had been intimate with *Rosa,* a married woman, and had oftentimes committed adultery with her, promising to marry her after the death of her husband. The husband died in 1732, but it was eight years later, in 1740, before *Raymundus* remembered his promise to

---

[17] S. C. C., January 15 and 19, July 2, 1718—in *Thesaurus Resolutionum Sacrae Congregationis Concilii,* vol. I, pp. 3, 7, 74

marry her. When the uncle and two sisters of *Raymundus* learned of his intention they did everything they could to prevent the marriage. *Rosa* was confined in a monastery and a judgment was placed in the archiepiscopal Curia which stated that the future spouses were guilty of two crimes, viz., of adultery and of the death of *Rosa's* husband. *Raymundus* and *Rosa,* however, obtained a dispensation from the Supreme Pontiff, after having testified that neither machinated in the death of her husband. The uncle and sisters of *Raymundus* then stated that the dispensation had been obtained surreptitiously, because the death of the husband was caused by the endeavor and deed of the wife. The Curia of the archdiocese did not heed their statement and declared that machination was not present, the Pontifical Brief was obtained and the marriage contracted without further delay. The uncle and sisters then took the case to the Sacred Congregation of the Council, where they again attempted to prove the crime of machination; but this was nullified *by the presumption of law* which excluded the crime; it was likewise nullified *by the testimony of many witnesses* who stated that the husband, *Carmel,* died of a tumor in the throat—among these witnesses being *Carmel's* own sister and her husband. Another witness was Januarius Sanseverinus, a *professor of medicine,* who had advised the dead man to live very carefully on account of the seriousness of his ailment, which would easily cause his death by strangulation. Two other doctors had already given him the same warning. The body of *Carmel* had lain unburied for forty-eight hours, during which time there appeared no indications that he had died a violent death.

The case was then proposed to the Sacred Congregation of the Council: (1) Is the impediment of crime, as stated, present in this case? (2) Should place be given to the execution of the Apostolic Letters regarding the dispensation in this case? The Congregation responded: *Negative ad primam partem, affirmative ad secundam.*[18]

Summing up the testimony as here considered, any kind of pertinent testimony will be acceptable as long as it contains a clear and certain proof. Prenuptial boastful threats or promise of marriage, motives of revenge rather than of marriage, shameful and continual co-habitation, extra-judicial confession, previous attempts at conjugicide, the testimony of doctors, all are found mentioned in the cases quoted, and are accepted or refused according to the weight of evidence they are able to bring.

---

[18] S. C. C. *in causa Neapolitana,* March 26, 1746—*in Thesaurus Resolutionum Sacrae Congregationis Concilii,* vol. XIII, pp. 144, 145.

CHAPTER VI

ADDENDA

§1. *Multiplication of the Impediment*

The impediment can be multiplied in two ways, from the viewpoint of the crime itself and from the viewpoint of the marriages involved:

(1) If the impediment arises from conjugicide alone, there is a double impediment when both accomplices are married and the spouse of each is slain.

(2) If the impediment arises from conjugicide with adultery, there is also a double impediment, and for the same reason.

(3) If the impediment arises from adultery with a promise of marriage or with an attempted marriage, there is a double impediment when both adulterers are married and both are aware of that circumstance;[1] also in the case of a married man who commits adultery with a girl and promises her marriage or attempts marriage with her and then, after the death of his wife, if he should marry still another and repeat the adultery and promise or attempt with the one with whom he has already contracted the impediment.[2]

(4) The impediment is multiplied also for the number of different crimes, if they differ in species, but not if they are of the same species and often committed during the same marriage, e. g., from adultery com-

[1] Vlaming, *Praelectiones Juris Matrimonii,* vol. I, n. 314.

[2] Gasparri, *De Matrimonio,* vol. I, n. 740.

mitted many times or from a promise or attempt often repeated.

(5) Hence the impediments can be so multiplied as to total two, four, six, etc., e. g., if Titius and Bertha are both married and, both being aware of that fact, they commit adultery and Titius promises her marriage, there are two impediments; if later, while his wife is still living, he attempts marriage with Bertha, there are four impediments; and further, if in order to take Bertha as his wife, he kills both her husband and his own wife, there are six impediments. And so other hypotheses can be made which would keep adding impediments to impediments.[3]

In seeking a dispensation from the impediment of crime, it is necessary that the circumstance of multiplicity be expressed, but it is not necessary, as Cappello advises, to indicate the number of impediments, because the best authors themselves cannot always determine that. It is oftentimes quite difficult to state just when a new impediment arises from an action, and thus it is sufficient to expose all the circumstances of the case.[4]

§ 2. *The Impediment for Orientals*

The spirit of the law among Orientals is that those guilty of conjugicide and of adultery between accomplices of the crime can never be admitted to marriage, and marriage is forbidden to them not only on account of the crime committed, but also from the presumption or suspicion of this crime. Thus, if one were accused of adultery, even tho he was not convicted, he could not marry his supposed accomplice. In the Oriental

---

[3] Vlaming, *Praelectiones Juris Matrimonii,* vol. I, n. 326; Gasparri, *De Matrimonio,* vol. I, n. 740.

[4] Cappello, *De Sacramentis,* vol. III, n. 500, 6.

Church the impediment of crime consists in this, that if a woman or a man commits adultery or conjugicide with the intention of later marrying the accomplice, such a marriage would be invalid.[5]

In the Synod of Mount Lebanon, held in the year 1736, the impediment of crime is found established just as clearly and definitely as in the legislation of the Latin Church. The Synod states that the two crimes, i. e., adultery and homicide (the slaying of one's spouse) do not always invalidate matrimony, but only in the following cases: (1) When a spouse commits adultery and afterwards efficaciously machinates in the death of his or her spouse for the purpose of contracting marriage with the accomplice of his adultery, the accomplice being aware of this and being a willing participant in the homicide or the adultery; (2) When, from the consent of both, a spouse is slain, even without adultery; (3) When adultery is committed and accompanied with a promise of marriage to take place after the death of the spouse still living, such a promise being accepted by the adulteress by words or some other external sign; (4) When one, whose spouse is still living, enters and consummates another marriage with his accomplice. The impediment is not contracted in this case if the accomplice is in good faith and does not know of the existence of the other spouse or if, upon discovering the truth, she abstains from further cohabitation with the adulterer.[6]

The law of the Latin Church is accepted by a majority of the various Eastern rites, e. g., the Syrians, Armenians, Egyptian Copts, but there are some who hold a law slightly different. The Ruthenians, in their

---

[5] Papp-Szilagyi, *Enchiridion Juris Ecclesiae Orientalis Catholicae*, p. 272, No. 117.

[6] Synod Mont. Libani, pars II, cap. XI- *Coll. Lac.*, tom. II, col. 164, 165.

Synod of the year 1720, state only the species of the impediment that arise from a promise concomitant with adultery or from machination of one of the accomplices, the other knowing, agreeing, and advising in the event of death of the innocent spouse.[7] Cappello states that this law of the Ruthenians is also accepted by the Chaldeans and Ethiopian Copts, while the Roumanians establish the diriment impediment only for conjugicide arising from mutual conspiracy and with only one of the parties possessing the intention of later contracting marriage. He further states that the impediment does not hold place among the Melchites, while the Orientals outside the true fold do not admit of such an impediment at all.[8]

§3. *The Impediment for Infidels*

Because the impediment of crime is of ecclesiastical law alone, the unbaptised are subject to it only indirectly, whereas all Christians, not only Catholics but also non-Catholics, are subjected to this law directly, unless otherwise exempted, e. g., heretics who marry among themselves are exempted from the form in the decree *Ne Temere.* In matrimonial cases the unbaptised, as has just been noted, are affected by the law of the Church only indirectly, and this for two reasons: (1) By reason of the dependence of the baptised person with whom the unbaptised wishes to contract marriage. The validity of the marriage contract requires the ability of both parties and consequently the inability directly affecting one party indirectly affects the other party also. This principle is clearly established in Canon 1036, § 3, which states that altho

[7] Synod Prov. Ruthenor., tit. IV, in *Coll. Lac.*, tom. II, col. 43.

[8] Cappello, *De Sacramentis,* vol. III, Appendix, art. III, n. 916.

the impediment exists on one side only, it nevertheless renders such a marriage illicit or invalid in so far as the impediment is impedient or diriment. (2) By reason of certain restraints contracted in infidelity. These restraints do not influence the validity of the marriage as long as the parties remain in infidelity but, after conversion, they constitute a diriment impediment.[9] Such restraints arise independently of the Church, viz., those that have their origin in nature, or are imposed by the law of the state.[10]

Neither in the previous ecclesiastical law nor in the Code does crime induce an impediment to marriage after Baptism, when based on a fact anterior to Baptism, for the restraint arising from the impediment of crime is considered as of ecclesiastical institution alone and cannot therefore be contracted while in the state of infidelity. Accordingly, a restraint of this kind cannot revive after Baptism and constitute an impediment and, as regards crime, it rests on a fault that is held to be blotted out by Baptism.[11]

In regard to the indirect influence of the Church over the unbaptised, two observations should be made: (1) In order that the baptised party may communicate to the unbaptised his own inability on the ground of crime, it is necessary that the baptised party himself should have committed the offense under the conditions required for contracting the impediment. This would be the case if, e. g., he had been guilty of the act of adultery alone (i. e., with a third party), and the murder had been committed by the unbaptised prospective partner alone; for adultery alone is not enough to constitute the impediment. It would be otherwise if the baptised person committed adultery

[9] De Becker, *De Sponsalibus et Matrimonio,* cap. II, p. 33.

[10] De Smet, *Betrothment and Marriage,* vol. I, n. 431.

[11] De Smet, *loc. cit.*

with the unbaptised and both promised matrimony, for in this case the double element of the impediment is present in the person of the baptised party, and the disability is communicated to the unbaptised party.[12] (2) A crime committed before Baptism does not acquire an invalidating force in respect to a marriage to be contracted after Baptism; not even if the Baptism took place, e. g., after the adultery and before the promise of marriage, or the attempt at marriage, or the murder. This would not be the case if the promise, attempt, or murder anterior to Baptism were confirmed after Baptism and accompanied by adultery; then the entire crime constituting the impediment would be considered as following Baptism.[13]

If, of the parties machinating in the death of the spouse, one is a Christian and the other is an infidel, and the purpose of their action is that the marriage between them may bring about the conversion of the infidel to the true faith, the impediment still prevents them from marriage, as was decided in the decree of Celestine III.[14] The question naturally arises: How can the Church include infidels, who are outside her jurisdiction, in this impediment and punish them for a crime committed in infidelity; and how is it that the penalty is not wiped out by Baptism, which wipes out all past sins? There are two solutions of the case, both satisfactory, tho not exhaustive. The first solution states that this impediment is common to both parties, the Christian and the infidel, but that while it ceases at Baptism—as far as the infidel party is concerned—nevertheless it still perdures for the Christian. The second solution states that while both sins and their penalties are wiped out by Baptism, impediments are

[12] Cf. Canon 1036, § 3.

[13] De Smet, *Betrothment and Marriage,* vol. II, n. 669.

[14] C. 1, X, *de conversione infidelium,* III, 33.

not. Neither solution, however, explains how the Church can state a penalty for infidels exempt from her jurisdiction, and both suppose that it is stated, and they only declare the manner in which this penalty is extinguished, viz., by Baptism. But it is the opinion of Sanchez that the infidel neither is nor can be included in this penalty, but the Christian party alone, so that the latter is perpetually prevented from marrying the former, even tho he be later converted to the faith. He quotes the parallel case of the impediment of the disparity of cult, in which the marriage of a Christian and an infidel contracted without the proper dispensation is invalid, not because the infidel is impeded, but because the Christian is affected by the legislation of the Church.[15]

An instruction of the Holy Office to the Vicar Apostolic of Central Oceania on December 18, 1872 declares the marriages of infidels true and valid—tho non-sacramental; and a decree of the Congregation of the Propaganda on August 23, 1852 sets the infidel parties without the pale of the Church and definitely establishes them beyond her jurisdiction:

(1) Vir infidelis qui ante baptismum copulam habuit cum infideli uxore alterius, cui, annuente muliere fidem de futuro matrimonio acceptante, mortem intulit, potestne post utriusque baptismum matrimonium inire cum dicta muliere?

(2) Possuntne hoc matrimonium contrahere si, quando patrarunt ista crimina, una pars fuerit christiana?

---

[15] Sanchez, *De Sancto Matrimonii Sacramento,* lib. VII, disp. LXXVIII, n. 3. This, of course, was the legislation of the Church prior to the promulgation of the Code.

Resp. (1) Affirmative. (2) Negative.[16]

If the infidel slays his wife in order to marry his Christian accomplice in adultery, and he does this with the consent of the Christian, the impediment prevents such a marriage, but if he did this of his own accord and without the knowledge of his accomplice, there is no impediment because she was not a party to the conjugicide and adultery alone does not constitute the impediment.[17]

§4. *Ignorance of the Impediment*

In the old law there was a controversy among the commentators as to whether or not ignorance excused from this impediment. Some held that it did excuse and freed both accomplices from its incurrence because the impediment took account of a punishment which was extraordinary in itself. But the more recognised commentators averred that it did not excuse because, as they claimed, this impediment is more of an incapability than a punishment, and even tho it was induced as a penalty ignorance does not excuse from it.[18]

In the case of ignorance on the part of one accomplice alone, the commentators holding the latter opinion admit that since the one aware of the impediment is bound directly the impediment affects the ignorant party only indirectly; but they except the case in which the ignorant party would be the adulterer and the

---

[16] *Collectanea de Prop. Fide,* n. 1300; cf. n. 1256.

[17] C. 1, X, *de conversione infidelium,* III, 33; Sanchez, *De Sancto Matrimonii Sacramento,* lib. VII, disp. LXXVIII, n. 4.

[18] Suarez, *Tractatus de Legibus,* lib. V, cap. 19; Schmalzgrueber, *Jus Ecclesiasticum Universum,* pars II, tit. VII, n. 59; Sanchez, *De Sancto Matrimonii Sacramento,* lib. IX, disp. XXXII, n. 17; Reiffenstuel, *Jus Canonicum Universum,* lib. IV, tit. VII, n. 26; Wernz, *Jus Decretalium,* tit. XXIII, n. 522.

murderer, as he would not be bound directly and consequently the other accomplice would be indirectly immune.[19]

In the Code it is certain that ignorance of this impediment does not excuse, as is clear from Canon 16 § 1, "Nulla ignorantia legum irritantium aut inhabilitantium ab eisdem excusat, nisi aliud expresse dicatur."

§5. *Cessation and Dispensation*

By its nature the impediment of crime is perpetual and can therefore be taken away only by means of a dispensation. But since it is merely of ecclesiastical origin in regard to each and every one of its species the Church can certainly dispense, even when it is a matter of conjugicide, whether the latter be occult or public. This is clear from the two Constitutions of Pope Benedict XIV, the *"Pastor Bonus"* of April 13, 1744 and the *"Aestas Anni"* of October 28, 1757.[20]

If the impediment is of public conjugicide, with one or the other or both accomplices machinating, the Holy See does not dispense. Benedict XIV, in the Constitution already cited, *"Aestas Anni,"* says, "Neque tamen exemplo ullo constat, Pontificem dispensasse in impedimento hujusmodi publico." If the impediment is of occult conjugicide the dispensation is granted for a most weighty cause but a salutary penance must be enjoined.[21]

It is sometimes difficult to establish an impediment as public. An impediment can be public in two ways: (1) by its nature, if it is based upon a fact *de se* public, e. g., consanguinity, affinity, holy orders, disparity of cult; or (2) by its circumstances, if the fact of itself

---

[19] Gasparri, *De Matrimonio,* vol. I, n. 748.

[20] *Bullarium,* vol. I, p. 361; vol. III, pars 2, p. 476.

[21] Gasparri, *De Matrimonio,* vol. I, n. 743.

is occult but has already been divulged, or it is so known that the divulgation of it is probable and it is possible to prove this divulgation in the external forum, e. g., the impediment of crime. Every notorious impediment is public but not every public impediment is notorious,[22] and thus the principal element to be considered in a public impediment is not the knowledge or divulgation as such but the proof of it in the external forum. As long as an impediment cannot be proven in the external forum it is considered occult even tho it is public by nature. An impediment can be materially public and formally occult, if the fact itself is known but there is no knowledge that an impediment arises from this fact, or if it is known that sexual intercourse was committed and a promise of marriage given, but it is not known that this crime was committed while a previous marriage endured.[23] In such a case the impediment must be considered as public despite the fact that it is not known that the impediment is incurred.[24]

If the impediment arises from adultery with a promise of marriage or with an attempted marriage the Holy See dispenses more readily, e. g., if a woman were to be defamed or to remain unmarried, if a public scandal would arise, etc., and the reason for this readiness of the Holy See to dispense here is gathered from the words of Canon 1042, § 2, 5°, which state that an impediment of this sort is of a minor degree only. When the adultery and the promise or attempted marriage are public a more weighty cause is demanded for the dispensation than when these are occult.[25]

---

[22] Canon 2197.

[23] Gasparri, *De Matrimonio,* vol. I, nn. 259, 260; Cappello, *De Sacramentis,* vol. III, n. 200.

[24] *Pont. Comm. Interpret.* in *Apollinaris,* I (1928), 245; Wernz-Vidal, *Jus Matrimoniale,* pars II, cap. I, p. 166, footnote 9.

[25] Wernz, *Jus Decretalium,* tit. XXIII, n. 534.

A dispensation granted by the Holy See for a marriage *ratum et non consummatum* or a permission granted by the same for entrance into another marriage on account of the presumed death of the spouse always contains—even when not expressly mentioned—a dispensation from the impediment arising from adultery with a promise of marriage or an attempted marriage, should such a dispensation be necessary, but it does not contain a dispensation from the impediment of crime when conjugicide is included.[26]

"Excepting the Roman Pontiff, no one can abrogate or derogate the impediments of ecclesiastical law, whether these impediments be impedient or diriment; neither can anyone dispense from them unless this power has been granted him by the common law or by a special Indult of the Apostolic See." [27]

Canons 1043, 1044, and 1045 grant certain powers of dispensing to bishops, priests, and confessors in some particular exigencies, and while it is not the purpose of this treatise to enter upon a detailed commentary of these canons (such commentary having already been treated by all modern authorities, as well as in this School of Canon Law),[28] nevertheless a brief resumé of their salient features might serve in regard to the impediment of crime.

Besides the more general power of dispensation granted to Ordinaries by Canons 81-86, special faculties are given in Canons 1043-1045 for the relief of conscience in urgent danger of death, provided all danger of scandal is removed. This power is now ordinary in so far as it is annexed to the office by law and it is granted to the local Ordinaries; hence religious

---

[26] Canon 1053.

[27] Canon 1040.

[28] Cf. O'Keeffe, *Matrimonial Dispensations*.

superiors are excluded.[29] The impediments which may be dispensed from are all the impediments of the ecclesiastical law—one of which is the impediment of crime—and it matters not whether these impediments are public or occult, diriment or impedient, with the sole exceptions of priesthood and affinity in the direct line. The power is personal to the Ordinary. It may be exercised by him not only in favor of his subjects, proper to him by the fact of domicile or quasi-domicile, but also in favor of those actually living in his territory. The same privilege enjoyed by Ordinaries in the Code is likewise granted to pastors, priests assisting at marriages, and confessors; the latter however only in the internal forum and in the act of sacramental confession. But all these enjoy the privilege only when it is impossible to present the case to the Ordinary.

The same powers are granted to Ordinaries, pastors, simple priests, and confessors in Canon 1045. The conditions and the impediments are the same as in the two preceding canons but the circumstances are different. Here the dispensation may be granted *if* everything is ready for the marriage and *if* the marriage cannot be postponed without the probable danger of a serious inconvenience until such time as the dispensation could be obtained from the Holy See.[30]

In the Quinquennial Faculties granted to Ordinaries there is granted the power of dispensing for a just and reasonable cause from the impediments of minor grade mentioned in Canon 1042, among which is included the impediment of crime arising from adultery with a promise of marriage or with an attempted marriage; likewise, the power of dispensing from the impediment of crime when it is occult and when machination is

[29] Canon 198.

[30] Vermeersch-Creusen, *Epitome Juris Canonici,* vol. I, nn. 305-312; Augustine, *A Commentary on Canon Law,* vol. V, 96-109.

lacking—and this whether the marriage is already contracted or is about to be contracted—having enjoined a fitting and salutary penance and, in the case of a marriage already contracted, having advised the supposed spouses of their obligation to renew their consent secretly.[31]

For the forms to be used in seeking dispensations, the reader is referred to the treatise "Betrothment and Marriage" of Canon A. De Smet, second edition, vol. II, supplement I, pp. 309-320.

§6. *Stated Penalties*

The impediment of crime cannot be classified as a real medicinal or vindicative penalty because no mention of it is made in the Code in the titles treating of these penalties.[32] That it is not a medicinal penalty is clear from the very concept of an impediment and of a medicinal penalty or censure. An impediment is a circumstance which prevents a licit or valid contraction of marriage,[33] while a censure is a punishment by which a baptised person who is delinquent and contumacious is deprived of spiritual goods or goods closely allied with the spiritual until such time as he departs from his obstinacy and is absolved.[34]

The impediment of crime cannot be called a vindicative penalty because such a penalty tends directly to the expiation of the crime committed, so that its forgiveness does not depend upon the cessation of the obstinacy of the delinquent party.[35]

---

[31] Cf. Quinquennial Faculties in Vermeersch-Creusen, *Epitome Juris Canonici*, vol. I, lib. II, Appendix III, p. 541. Cf. also Faculties of Apostolic Delegate, *loc. cit.*, Appendix I, p. 525.

[32] Cf. Book V, pars II, tits. VIII, IX.

[33] Cappello, *De Sacramentis*, vol. III, n. 195.

[34] Canon 2241, § 1.

[35] Canon 2286.

In regard to this impediment no special and definite penalties are specifically drawn up, but there are some penalties established for the several crimes of adultery, bigamy, and homicide, all of which classifications can be included in the ecclesiastical impediment which it is customary to nominate as crime. Canon 2357 § 2 excludes all those guilty of public adultery from all legitimate ecclesiastical acts until such time as they recede from their delinquency; these ecclesiastical acts are enumerated in Canon 2256, 2°. Canon 2356 states that bigamists, those who attempt another marriage while still bound by one already existing, are *ipso facto* brought into ill repute and if they persist in their illicit relationships, they are to be excommunicated and inflicted with a personal interdict according to the gravity of their sin. Canon 2354 § 1 excludes laics *ipso jure* from legitimate ecclesiastical acts and from any offices they might have held in the Church and imposes the added burden of making restitution for the injury caused by them. In the ancient law of the Church those who were guilty of conjugicide were forbidden, on account of the great malice of their action, to enter the state of matrimony with any person whatsoever by force of an impeding impediment, but this penal sanction was taken away by contrary custom long before the Code was promulgated. In the *Decretum Gratiani* there are discovered letters, one from Pope Nicholas I to Archbishop Rudolph of Bourges in which men who slay their wives are placed under interdict; and one from Pope Stephen V to a man by the name of Astulphus who had also slain his wife. Pope Stephen suggests to him penance in a monastery or, at his own choice, public penance, abstinence from wine and meat, a diet of bread, water and salt, vigils, prayers, almsgiving, etc.[36] In canon 5 of the National Council of

Vermerie, held under Pepin in the year 753, it was decreed that homicide brought about thru self-defense did not prevent such a murderer from entering marriage again after the death of his first wife.[87]

[86] C. 5, 8, C. XXXIII, q. 2.

[87] C. 1, X, *de divortiis,* IV, 19.

BIBLIOGRAPHY

SOURCES

Acta Apostolicae Sedis, Commentarium Officiale, Romae, 1909.

Acta Sanctae Sedis, 41 vols., Romae, 1865-1908.

Acta et Decreta Sacrorum Consiliorum Recentiorum (Collectio Lacensis), 7 vols., Friburgi Brisgoviae, 1870-1890.

Bullarium Diplomatum et Privilegiorum Sanctorum Pontificum Taurinensis editio, auspicante Cardinali Francisco Gaude, 25 vols., Augustae Taurinorum, 1857-1872.

Canones et Decreta Sacrosancti Oecomenici Concilii Tridentini, Neapoli, 1859.

Code of Hammurabi, King of Babylon, edited by Robert Francis Harper, 2 ed., Chicago, 1904.

Codex Juris Canonici Pii X Pontificis Maximi iussu digestus Benedicti Papae XV auctoritate promulgatus, Praefatione, Fontium Annotatione et Indice Analytico Alphabetico ab Emo Petro Card. Gasparri Auctus, Romae, 1918.

Codex Theodosianus, Ed. P. Krueger, Th. Mommsen, P. M. Meyer, 3 vols., Berolini, 1905.

Codicis Juris Canonici Fontes, cura Emi Petri Gasparri editi, 4 vols., Romae, 1925-1928.

Collectanea S. Congregationis de Propagande Fide, 2 vols., Romae, 1907.

Corpus Juris Canonici, Editio Lipsiensis II (Richter-Friedberg), 2 vols., Lipsiae, 1922.

Corpus Juris Civilis, 3 vols., Berolini, 1928-1929.

Hardouin, Jean, *Acta Conciliorum et Epistolae Decretales ac Constitutiones Summorum Pontificum,* 12 vols., Parisiis, 1715.

Holy Bible, Douay Version, Baltimore, 1914.

Mansi, Joannes Dominicus, *Sacrorum Conciliarum Nova et Amplissima Collectio,* 51 vols., Florentiae, 1859.

Martin, Conrad, *Collectio Documentorum Omnium Concilii Vaticani,* Paderborn, 1873.

Regulae Cancellariae Apostolicae, Joannes XXII—Nicolaus V, Innsbruck, 1888.

Riccobono, Salvator, *Fontes Juris Romani Antejustiniani,* Florentiae, 1909.

Sacrae Romanae Rotae Decisiones seu Sententiae, 8 vols., and appendix, Romae, 1761.

Synodus Sciarfensis Syrorum, Romae, 1897.
Thesaurus Resolutionum Sacrae Congregationis Concilii, 167 vols., Romae, 1718-1908.

AUTHORS

Alphonsus, M. de Ligorio, *Theologia Moralis,* 5 vols., Taurini, 1872.
Anselms von Laon, *Systematiche Sentenzen,* Münster, 1919.
Ayrinhac, H. A., *Marriage Legislation in the New Code of Canon Law,* New York, 1918.
[Bachofen], Charles Augustine, *A Commentary on the New Code of Canon Law,* 8 vols., St. Louis, 1923-1929; Vol. I, 5 ed., 1926; Vol. II, 5 ed., 1928; Vol. III, 4 ed., 1929; Vol. IV, 3 ed., 1925; Vol. V. 4 ed., 1929; Vol. VI, 2. ed., 1923; Vol. VII, 2. ed., 1923; Vol. VIII, 2. ed., 1924.
Barbosa, Augustinus, *Collectanea Doctorum tam Veterum quam Recentiorum in Jus Pontificium Universum,* Lugduni, 1658.
Bellarminus, Robertus, *Opera Omnia ex Editione Veneta, iterum editit Justinus Fevre,* 12 vols., *Parisiis,* 1870-1874.
Bertachini, *Repertorium Joannis Bertachini,* Venetiis, 1570.
Cappello, Felix M., *Tractatus Canonico-Moralis de Sacramentis,* Vol., III, *De Matrimonio,* 2 ed., Romae, 1927.
Catholic Encyclopedia, The, 17 vols., New York, 1907-1922.
Cathrein, Victor, *Moralphilosophie,* 6 ed., 2 vols., Leipsig, 1924.
Cerato, Prosdocimus, *Matrimonium a Codice Juris Canonici integre desumptum,* 4 ed., Patavii, 1927.
Chelodi, Joannes, *Jus Matrimoniale,* 3 ed., Tridenti, 1921.
Corbett, Percy Ellwood, *The Roman Law of Marriage,* Oxford, 1930.
Costa, Emilio, *Crimini e Pene da Romolo a Giustiniano,* Bologna, 1921.
Cronin, Michael, *The Science of Ethics,* 2 vols., New York, 1920.
De Angelis, Phillipus, *Praelectiones Juris Canonici ad Methodum Decretalium* Gregorii IX Exactae, 6 vols., Romae, 1887.
De Becker, Julius, *De Sponsalibus et Matrimonio Praelectiones Canonicae,* Brussels, 1896.
De Smet, A., *Betrothment and Marriage,* 2 ed., 2 vols., Bruges, 1925.
Farrugia, Nicolaus, *De Matrimonio et Causis Matrimonialibus Tractatus Canonico-Moralis juxta Codicem Juris Canonici,* Taurini-Romae, 1924.
Ferreres, Joannes B., *Casus Conscientiae,* 5 ed., (2a post Codicem), 2 vols., Barcinone, 1926.
Gasparri, Petrus, *Tractatus Canonicus de Matrimonio,* 3 ed., 2 vols., Parisiis, 1904.
Genicot, Eduardus, *Theologiae Moralis Institutiones,* 2 vols, Lovanii, 1897.
Giraldus, Ubaldus, *Expositio Juris Pontificii,* Romae, 1829.
Hunter, William A., *Introduction to Roman Law,* London, 1908.

Laymann, Paulus, *Theologiae Moralis in Quinque Libros Partitae,* Venetiis, 1719.

Lega, Michael, *Praelectiones in Textum Juris Canonici de Judiciis Ecclesiasticis,* vol. I, Romae, 1896.

Liebell, J. F., *Readings in Ethics,* Chicago, 1926.

Leurenius, Petrus, *Jus Canonicum Universum,* 5 vols., Venetiis, 1729.

Mansella, Joseph, *De Impedimentis Matrimonium Dirimentibus ac de Processu Judiciali in Causis Matrimonialibus,* Romae, 1881.

Maroto, Philippus, *Institutiones Juris Canonici ad Norman Novi Codicis,* 2 vols., Romae, 1919-1921.—Vol. I, 3 ed., Romae, 1921; Vol. II, Romae, 1919.

Marrero, I, *Tradado del Impedimento Dirimente del Matrimonio Denominado Crimen,* Washington, 1917.

Migne, Jacques Paul, *Patrologiae Cursus Completus—Series Latina,* 221 vols., Parisiis, 1844-1855.

Mommsen, Theodor, *Le Droit Penal Romain, Paris,* 1907.

Morey, William C., *Outlines of Roman Law,* New York and London, 1914.

Motry, Hubert L., *Diocesan Faculties according to the Code of Canon Law,* Washington, 1922.

Neuberger, Nicholas J., *Canon 6, or the Relation of the Codex Juris Canonici* to *Preceding Legislation,* Washington, 1927.

Noldin, H., *Summa Theologiae Moralis,* 21 ed., 3 vols., Oeniponte, 1928.

O'Keeffe, Gerald M., *Matrimonial Dispensations, Powers of Bishops, Priests, and Confessors,* Washington, 1927.

Ojetti, Benedictus, *Synopsis Rerum Moralium et Juris Pontificii,* 4 vols., Romae, 1909.

Pallottini, Salvator, *Collectio Omnium Conclusionum et Resolutionum quae in causis propositis apud S. Cong. Cardinalium S. Concilii Tridentini Interpretum prodierunt ab anno 1564 ad annum 1860,* 17 vols., Romae, 1868-1893.

Papp-Szilagyi, Joseph, *Enchiridion Juris Ecclesiae Orientalis Catholicae,* Hollosoy-Magno Varadini, 1880.

Perrone, Joannes, *De Matrimonio Christiano,* 3 vols., Romae, 1858.

Pirhing, Ernricus, *Jus Canonicum Nova Methodo Explicatum,* 2 vols., Dilingae, 1678.

Raymond de Pennafort, *Summa,* Veronae, 1744.

Reiffenstuel, Anacletus, *Jus Canonicum Universum,* 4 vols., Venetiis, 1735.

Roberti, Franciscus, *De Processibus,* 2 vols., Romae, 1926.

Sanchez, Thomas, *De Sancto Matrimonii Sacramento Disputationum,* Venetiis, 1693.

Schmalzgrueber, Franciscus, *Jus Ecclesiasticum Universum,* 12 vols., Romae, 1844.

Smith, S. B., *Elements of Ecclesiastical Law,* 2 vols., New York, 1882.

Sohm, Rudolph, *History and System of Roman Private Law,* Oxford, 1926.

Staudt, Sylvester P., *Knowableness of Natural Law,* Washington, 1926.

Strachan-Davidson, James Leigh, *Problems of the Roman Criminal Law,* Oxford, 1912.

Suarez, Franciscus, *Tractatus de Legibus ac Deo Legislatore,* Lugduni, 1619.

Thomas Aquinas, *Commentaria in Quartos Libros Sententiarum Petri Lombardi,* Parisiis, 1659.

Thomas Aquinas, *Summa Theologica,* 17 ed. Taurinensis, 6 vols., Taurini, 1922.

Tiraquelli, Andreas, *De Legibus Connubialibus et Jure Maritali,* Lugdini, 1569.

Van Espen, Z. B., *Opera Omnia,* Venetiis, 1766.

Vermeersch-Creusen, *Epitome Juris Canonici,* 4 ed., 3 vols., Mechliniae-Romae, 1929.

Vlaming, Th. M., *Praelectiones Juris Matrimonii ad Norman Codicis Juris Canonici,* 3 ed., 2 vols., Bussum in Hollandia, 1921.

Von Pornaxio, Raphael-Michel, Karl, *Der Liber de Consonancia Nature et Gracie,* Münster, 1915.

Wernz, Franciscus, *Jus Decretalium,* 2 ed., 6 vols., Prati, 1912.

Wernz, Franciscus—Vidal, Petrus, *Jus Canonicum ad Codicis Norman Exactum,* 3 vols., Romae, 1927-1928.

Westermarck, Edward, *The History of Human Marriage,* London, 1891.

PERIODICALS

Apollinaris, Romae, 1928-

Archiv für katholisches Kirchenrecht, vol. I, Innsbruck, 1857.

Theologische Quartalschrift, Tübingen, 1819-

Theologisch-praktische Quartalschrift, Linz, 1832-

veitschrift für katholische Theologie, Innsbruck, 1877-

Universitas Catholica Americae

Washingtonii, D. C.

Facultas Juris Canonici

1931

No. 69

DEUS LUX MEA.

TITULI

QUOS

AD DOCTORATUS GRADUM

IN

JURE CANONICO

APUD UNIVERSITATEM CATHOLICAM AMERICAE

CONSEQUENDUM

PUBLICE PROPUGNABIT

JOANNES FRANCISCUS DONOHUE

SACERDOS DIOECESIS BUFFALENSIS

JURIS CANONICI LICENTIATUS

HORA XI A.M. DIE XXV MAII MCMXXXI

TITULI

IN IURE CANONICO

I.	De Dissertatione.	
II.	De Historia Iuris Canonici.	
III.	Canones 1-7	De Ambitu Codicis.
IV.	Canones 8-24	De Legibus Ecclesiasticis.
V.	Canones 25-30	De Consuetudine.
VI.	Canones 31-25	De Temporis Supputatione.
VII.	Canones 36-62	De Rescriptis.
VIII.	Canones 63-79	De Privilegiis.
IX.	Canones 80-86	De Dispensationibus.
X.	Canones 87-107	Generalis Notiones de Personis.
XI.	Canones 111-117	De Clericorum Adscriptione Alicui Dioecesi.
XII.	Canones 118-123	De Iuribus et Privilegiis Clericorum
XIII.	Canones 124-144	De Obligationibus Clericorum.
XIV.	Canones 145-195	De Officiis Ecclesiasticis.
XV.	Canones 196-210	De Potestate Ordinaria et Delegata.
XVI.	Canones 487-498	De Notione Religionis, et de Erectione et Suppressione Religionis, Provinciae, Domus.
XVII.	Canones 499-537	De Religionum Regimine.
XVIII.	Canones 538-586	De Admissione in Religionem.
XIX.	Canones 673-681	De Societatibus sive Virorum sive Mulierum in Communi Viventium sine Votis.
XX.	Canones 1012-1018	De Matrimonio in Genere.
XXI.	Canones 1019-1034	De Iis quae Matrimonii Celebrationi Praemitti debent.
XXII.	Canones 1035-1057	De Impedimentis in Genere.
XXIII.	Canones 1058-1066	De Impedimentis Impedientibus.
XXIV.	Canones 1067-1080	De Impedimentis Dirimentibus.
XXV.	Canones 1081-1093	De Consensu Matrimoniali.
XXVI.	Canones 1552-1568	De Notione Iudicii et de Foro Competenti.
XXVII.	Canones 1569-1607	De Variis Tribunalium Gradibus et Speciebus.
XXVIII.	Canones 1608-1645	De Disciplina in Tribunalibus Servanda.

XXIX. Canones 1646-1666 De Partibus in Causa.
XXX. Canones 1667-1705 De Actionibus et Exceptionibus.
XXXI. Canones 1706-1725 De Causae Introductione.
XXXII. Canones 1726-1746 De Litis Contestatione, de Litis Instantia, et de Interrogationibus Partibus in Iudicio Faciendis.
XXXIII. Canones 1747-1836 De Probationibus.
XXXIV. Canones 1837-1857 De Causis Incidentibus.
XXXV. Canones 1858-1877 De Processus Publicatione, de Conclusione in Causa, de Causae Discussione, et de Sententia.
XXXVI. Canones 1879-1891 De Appellatione.
XXXVII. Canones 1902-1907 De Re Iudicata et de Restitutione in Integrum.
XXXVIII. Canones 1960-1992 De Causis Matrimonialibus.
XXXIX. Canones 2195-2198 De Natura Delicti eiusque Divisione.
XL. Canones 2199-2211 De Imputabilitate Delicti, de Causis illam Aggravantibus vel Minuentibus, et de Iuridicis Delicti Effectibus.
XLI. Canones 2212-2213 De Conatu Delicti.
XLII. Canones 2214-2240 De Poenis in Genere.
XLIII. Canones 2241-2285 De Poenis Medicinalibus seu de Censuris.
XLIV. Canones 2286-2305 De Poenis Vindicativis.
XLV. Canones 2306-2313 De Remediis Poenalibus et Poenitentiis.

IN IURE ROMANO

XLVI. The Periods of Roman Law.
XLVII. The Sources of Roman Law.
XLVIII. Personality.
XLIX. Slavery.
L. Citizenship.
LI. Patria Potestas.
LII. Personae in Manu.
LIII. Tutela et Cura.
LIV. Personae in Mancipio.
LV. Ownership.
LVI. De Obligationibus in Genere.
LVII. De Obligationibus Extra-Contractualibus.
LVIII. Furtum.
LIX. Damnum Injuria Datum.
LX. Injuria.

Vidit Facultas:

VALENTINUS T. SCHAAF, O.F.M., J.C.D., Vice-Decanus.

LUDOVICUS H. MOTRY, S.T.D., J.C.D., a Secretis.

FRANCISCUS J. LARDONE, S.T.D., J.U.D.

Vidit Rector Magnificus Universitatis:

JACOBUS HUGO RYAN, S.T.D., Ph.D., LL.D., Litt.D.

VITA.

John Francis Donohue was born in Buffalo, N. Y. on November 16, 1897. He attended Public School 33, St. Stephen's parochial school, Canisius High School, all of that city, Niagara University, and the Seminary of Our Lady of Angels at Niagara Falls, N. Y. He received the degrees of A.B. and M.A. from Niagara University, and was ordained on January 25, 1927. In September 1929 he entered the Catholic University of America at Washington, D. C., registering in the School of Canon Law.

CATHOLIC UNIVERSITY OF AMERICA

CANON LAW STUDIES

1. Freriks, Rev. Celestine A., C.PP.S., J.C.D., Religious Congregations in Their External Relations, 121 pp., 1916.
2. Galliher, Rev. Daniel M., O.P., J.C.D., Canonical Elections, 117 pp., 1917
3. Borkowski, Rev. Aurelius L., O.F.M., J.C.D., De Confraternitatibus Ecclesiasticis, 136 pp., 1918.
4. Castillo, Rev. Cayo, J.C.D., Disertacion Historico-canonica sobre la Potestad del Cabildo en Sede Vacante o Impedida del Vicario Capitular, 99 pp., 1919 (1918).
5. Kubelbeck, Rev. William J., S.T.B., J.C.D., The Sacred Penitentiaria and Its Relations to Faculties of Ordinaries and Priests, 129 pp., 1918.
6. Petrovits, Rev. Joseph J. C., S.T.D., J.C.D., The New Church Law on Matrimony, X-461 pp., 1919.
7. Hickey, Rev. John J., S.T.B., J.C.D., Irregularities and Simple Impediments in the New Code of Canon Law, 100 pp., 1920.
8. Klekotka, Rev. Peter J., S.T.B., J.C.D., Diocesan Consultors, 179 pp., 1920.
9. Wannenmacher, Rev. Francis, J.C.D., The Evidence in Ecclesiastical Procedure Affecting the Marriage Bond, 1920. (Not Printed.)
10. Golden, Rev. Henry Francis, J.C.D., Parochial Benefices in the New Code, IV-119 pp., 1921. (Printed 1925.)
11. Koudelka, Rev. Charles J., J.C.D., Pastors, Their Rights and Duties According to the New Code of Canon Law, 211 pp., 1921.
12. Melo, Rev. Antonius, O.F.M., J.C.D., De Exemptione Regularium, X-188 pp., 1921.
13. Schaaf, Rev. Valetine Theodore, O.F.M., S.T.B., J.C.D., The Cloister, X-180 pp., 1921.
14. Burke, Rev. Thomas Joseph, S.T.B., J.C.D., Competence in Ecclesiastical Tribunals, IV-117 pp., 1922.
15 Leech, Rev. George Leo, J.C.D., A Comparative Study of the Constitution "Apostolicae Sedis" and the "Codex Juris Canonici," 179 pp., 1922.

16. Motry, Rev. Hubert Louis, S.T.D., J.C.D., Diocesan Faculties according to the Code of Canon Law, II-167 pp., 1922.
17. Murphy, Rev. George Lawrence, J.C.D., Delinquencies and Penalties in the Administration and the Reception of the Sacraments, IV-121 pp., 1923.
18. O'Reilly, Rev. John Anthony, S.T.B., J.C.D., Ecclesiastical Sepulture in the New Code of Canon Law, II-129 pp., 1923.
19. Michalicka, Rev. Wenceslas Cyrill, O.S.B., J.C.D., Judicial Procedure in Dismissal of Clerical Exempt Religious, 107 pp., 1923.
20. Dargin, Rev. Edward Vincent, S.T.B., J.C.D., Reserved Cases According to the Code of Canon Law, IV-103 pp., 1924.
21. Godfrey, Rev. John A., S.T.B., J.C.D., The Right of Patronage According to the Code of Canon Law, 153 pp., 1924.
22. Hagedorn, Rev. Francis Edward, J.C.D., General Legislation on Indulgences, II-154 pp., 1924.
23. King, Rev. James Ignatius, J.C.D., The Administration of the Sacraments to Dying Non-Catholics, V-141 pp., 1924.
24. Winsow, Rev. Francis Joseph, A.F.M., J.C.D., Vicars and Prefects Apostolic, IV-149 pp., 1924.
25. Correa, Rev. Jose Servelion, S.T.L., J.C.D., La Potestad Legislativa de la Iglesia Catolica, IV-127 pp., 1925.
26. Dugan, Rev. Henry Francis, M.A., J.C.D., The Judiciary Department of the Diocesan Curia, 87 pp., 1925.
27. Keller, Rev. Charles Frederick, S.T.B., J.C.D., Mass Stipends, 167 pp., 1925.
28. Paschang, Rev. John Linus, J.C.D., The Sacramentals According to the Code of Canon Law, 129 pp., 1925.
29. Piontek, Rev. Cyrillus, O.F.M., S.T.B., J.C.D., De Indulto Exclaustrationis necnon Saecularizationis, XIII-289 pp., 1925.
30. Kearney, Rev. Richard Joseph, S.T.B., J.C.D., Sponsors at Baptism According to the Code of Canon Law, IV-127 pp., 1925.
31. Bartlett, Rev. Chester Joseph, A.M., LL.B., J.C.D., The Tenure of Parochial Property in the United States of America, V-108 pp., 1926.
32. Kilker, Rev. Adrian Jerome, J.C.D., Extreme Unction, V-425 pp., 1926.
33. McCormick, Rev. Robert Emmett, J.C.D., Confessors of Religious, VIII-266 pp., 1926.
34. Miller, Rev. Newton Thomas, J.C.D., Founded Masses According to the Code of Canon Law, VII-93 pp., 1926.
35. Roelker, Rev. Edward G., S.T.D., J.C.D., Principles of Privilege According to the Code of Canon Law, XI-166 pp., 1926.
36. Bakalarczyk, Rev. Richardus, M.I.C., J.U.D., De Novitiatu, VIII-208 pp., 1927.
37. Pizzuti, Rev. Lawrence, O.F.M., J.U.L., De Parochis Religiosis, 1927. (Not Printed.)

38. Bliley, Rev. Nicholas Martin, O.S.B., J.C.D., Altars According to the Code of Canon Law, XIX-132 pp., 1927.
39. Brown, Brendan Francis, A.B., LL.M., J.U.D., The Canonical Juristic Personality with Special Reference to its Status in the United States of America, V-212 pp., 1927.
40. Cavanaugh, Rev. William Thomas, C.P., J.U.D., The Reservation of the Blessed Sacrament, VIII-101 pp., 1927.
41. Doheny, Rev. William J., C.S.C., A.B., J.U.D., Church Property: Modes of Acquisition, X-118 pp., 1927.
42. Feldhaus, Rev. Aloysius H., C.PP.S., J.C.D., Oratories, IX-141 pp., 1927.
43. Kelly, Rev. James Patrick, A.B., J.C.D., The Jurisdiction of the Simple Confessor, X-208 pp., 1927.
44. Neuberger, Rev. Nicholas J., J.C.D., Canon 6 or the Relation of the Codex Juris Canonici to the Preceding Legislation, V-95 pp., 1927.
45. O'Keeffe, Rev. Gerald Michael, J.C.D., Matrimonial Dispensations, Powers of Bishops, Priests, and Confessors, VIII-232 pp., 1927.
46. Quigley, Rev. Joseph, A.M., A.B., J.C.D., Condemned Societies, 139 pp., 1927.
47. Zaplotnik, Rev. Ioannes Leo, J.C.D, De Vicariis Foraneis, X-142, 1927
48. Duskie, Rev. John Aloysius, A.B., J.C.D., The Canonical Status of the Orientals in the United States, VIII-196 pp., 1928.
49. Hyland, Rev. Francis Edward, J.C.D., Excommunication, Its Nature, Historical Development and Effects, VIII-181 pp., 1928.
50. Reinmann, Rev. Gerald Joseph, O.M.C., J.C.D., The Third Order Secular of Saint Francis, 201 pp., 1928.
51. Schenk, Rev. Francis J., J.C.D., The Matrimonial Impediments of Mixed Religion and Disparity of Cult. XVI-318 pp., 1929.
52. Coady, Rev. John Joseph, S.T.D., J.U.D., A.M., The Appointment of Pastors, VIII-150 pp., 1929.
53. Kay, Rev. Thomas Henry, J.C.D., Competence in Matrimonial Procedure, VIII-164 pp., 1929.
54. Turner, Rev. Sidney Joseph, C.P., J.U.D., The Vow of Poverty, XLIX-217 pp., 1929.
55. Kearney, Rev. Raymond A., A.B., S.T.D., J.C.D., The Principles of Delegation, VII-149 pp., 1929.
56. Conran, Rev. Edward James, A.B., J.C.D., The Interdict, V-163 pp., 1930.
57. O'Neill, Rev. William H., J.C.D., Papal Rescripts of Favor, VII-219 pp., 1930.
58. Bastnagel, Rev. Clement Vincent J.U.D., The Appointment of Parochial Adjutants and Assistants, XV-262 pp., 1930.

59. Ferry, Rev. William A., A.B., J.C.D., Stole Fees, X-108 pp., 1930.
60. Costello, Rev. John Michael, A.B., J.C.D., Domicile and Quasi-Domicile, VII-201 pp., 1930.
61. Kremer, Rev. Michael Nicholas, A.B., S.T.B., J.C.D., Church Support in the United States, VI-137 pp., 1930.
62. Angulo, Rev. Luis, C.M., J.C.L., Legislación de la Iglesia Católica sobre la intención en la aplicación de la Misa, 1931.
63. Frey, Rev. Wolfgang, O.S.B., A.B., J.C.L., The Act of Religious Profession, 1931.
64. Roberts, Rev. James Brendan, A.B., J.C.L., The Banns of Marriage, 1931.
65. Ryder, Rev. Raymond Aloysius, A.B., J.C.L., Simony, 1931.
66. Campagna, Rev. Michael Angelo, Ph.B., J.U.L., Il Vicario Generale del Vescovo, 1931.
67. Cox, Rev. Joseph Godfrey, A.B., J.C.L., The Administration of Seminaries, 1931.
68. Gregory, Rev. Donald Joseph, S.T.B., J.U.L., The Pauline Privilege, 1931.
69. Donohue, Rev. John Francis, A.M., J.C.L., The Impediment of Crime, 1931.
70. Dooley, Rev. Eugene A., O.M.Q., J.C.L., Church Law on Sacred Relics, 1931.

www.ingramcontent.com/pod-product-compliance
Lightning Source LLC
LaVergne TN
LVHW050202080826
844660LV00012B/334

* 9 7 8 0 8 1 3 2 2 2 5 8 5 *